# CAUGHT IN THE MIDDLE

D0454273

# CAUGHT
# IN THE
# MIDDLE

## BEVERLY BUSH SMITH
## AND PATRICIA DEVORSS

 5176

Tyndale House
Publishers, Inc.
Wheaton, Illinois

Unless otherwise noted, all Scripture references
are from *The Holy Bible,* New International
Version, copyright ©1973, 1978, 1984
International Bible Society. Used by permission
of Zondervan Bible Publishers.

Library of Congress Catalog Card Number 88-50085
ISBN 0-8423-0355-3
Copyright ©1988 by Beverly Bush Smith and Patricia DeVorss
Printed in the United States of America

95
8   7   6   5

# CONTENTS

# INTRODUCTION

God has blessed me with a terrific husband and the assurance that he is the perfect mate for me (not a perfect person, mind you, but precisely the right person for me). The fact that he is not yet a believer does not in any way diminish my love for him nor my trust that this is part of God's perfect plan for our growth, both individually and as a couple.

Now, I could not have written the preceding paragraph a few years ago. It was only after a lengthy season of doubting, agonizing, questioning, and, most important, studying God's Word and praying, that I arrived at this point of peace.

I was delighted to find a similar sense of contentment in Pat DeVorss, after she had a much longer and more intense struggle, which has yielded both insight and wisdom. She had been a Christian wife of an unbeliever for thirty years, as compared with my meager eleven.

Of course, we still have times of struggle, but as we looked around us, we found that our overall sense of satisfaction is far from universal. In fact, four women, one of whom has been waiting for twenty-eight years for her husband to receive the gift of faith, came to me within a single month and admitted, "I'm so down. I don't know how much longer I can handle this."

Some of them had solid marriages with good communication in every realm except the spiritual. One had numerous other problems to overcome.

These were the seeds of this book, which we see as a survival guide for the wife who lives with either an unsaved husband or a husband who seems considerably less committed in his faith than his spouse.

It is for the woman who sometimes finds herself wondering if she can continue this way, who feels guilty when she succumbs to the loneliness and sometimes the hopelessness of making her Christian walk without the person she most loves at her side.

This, then, is not a how-to-love-your-husband-to-the-Lord book, nor is it a woe-is-me professional martyr's manual. It is a practical, tell-it-like-it-is, here's-how-I-keep-going book, based on the experience of scores of wives of nonbelievers and barely believers.

We hope that it will give you a new sense of peace, hope, and empathy for your husband, and that, as Paul wrote, you will know the assurance that in whatever state you are, you can be content (Phil. 4:11).

*Beverly Bush Smith*

# ONE
# SOMETIMES I FEEL
# SO LONELY

With the children settled into Sunday school, Bette stands alone in the door of the sanctuary, feeling conspicuous, wondering where she should sit this time. Everywhere she looks, she sees couples. At last, she spots a husband and wife she knows. Taking a deep breath, she strides toward them and asks if she may sit with them. However, after greeting her, they turn their attention back to each other.

The service begins. She watches the wife and husband ahead of her reach spontaneously, affectionately for one another's hands. The man next to her puts his arm around his wife as they pray. Bette thinks of the husband she left at home, still in his bathrobe, reading the comic section of the Sunday paper.

"If only . . . ," she thinks, closing her eyes as they fill with tears.

## LONELINESS AT CHURCH

For thousands of wives, Sunday morning can be the loneliest time of the week, for it acutely emphasizes the sharing they do not have in their marriages to unbelieving and barely believing husbands.

Loneliness, in fact, is the word we heard most often when

we asked these women about the emotions they found most difficult to handle.

One woman, married twenty-nine years to an unbeliever, expressed it this way:

"I'd arrived early that Sunday morning. Only a few people were in church. Those I knew were already seated with their families, and I didn't want to intrude, so I decided to sit alone in hope that someone would choose to join me.

"Soon the rows around me filled with people, but no one sat in my row. I had carefully left two seats on the aisle for a couple, but no one stopped.

"I began to feel like an untouchable—so alone, so unloved that I even doubted my self-worth. I'm a leader in the women's ministries. I know a lot of people at church and teach a Bible study, but no one wanted to sit next to me. Maybe no one liked me. I tried so hard to be loving to others, but now . . .

"Finally, my heart leaped as a couple crossed in front of me to sit in my row. I quickly picked up my Bible from the seat beside me to make room, but they left the seat vacant anyway. I felt even more alone.

"Just as the service began, a couple sat on the aisle, perhaps not because they wanted to be next to me, but because those were the only handy seats left. Still, it was good to have company.

"Several times in the service my aloneness intensified—especially when the minister told the congregation to greet one another, and the couples on each side of me turned to others before they at last recognized me.

"This was the first time in many years that I had allowed myself to feel the intensity of my aloneness. It was painful, frightening. I promised myself that next Sunday I'd find someone to sit with, rather than hoping for someone to find me."

But another woman expressed what she considered "an even greater loneliness. It's having my husband beside me in church and feeling so excited about what I'm hearing, and seeing that he's dropping off to sleep. He's just not getting it at all! You don't have to be alone to be lonely," she reminded us.

Some wives find their biggest problem with loneliness at church functions, such as picnics and Christmas dinners. These festivities, which are so often couple-oriented, reinforce that "I don't belong" feeling. At such an affair, one woman recalls being asked to move three times to make room at a table for a couple.

Such forms of rebuff are difficult for anyone, but they may be shattering for a woman who is naturally shy. Some find it so overwhelming that they seldom or never go to church.

A number of women expressed feelings of loneliness and helplessness after they attended seminars or heard sermons targeted at couples. For instance, when the speaker holds up as an ideal the "family altar" or devotional time with the husband presiding, many of us despair that this will never happen in our homes.

Or, as Marie said sarcastically, "Thanks a lot! Now I know all the things my husband should be doing and isn't. The truth is, he can't, and I can't make him do it. These approaches and attitudes are totally out of his realm of experience. Instead of finding some answers, now I'm more frustrated than ever."

Well-meaning church friends may also unwittingly feed our loneliness with such suggestions as, "Wouldn't your husband love to come to our couples' Bible study?" Or, "You are bringing your husband to the potluck next Sunday, aren't you? It's going to be great."

The implication seems to be that if we would just ask him in the "right" way, surely he couldn't resist. That hurts when we know he has no desire to go. We want so much to be there, yet not alone—not without him. Or if he grudgingly consents to attend, his body is there, but he is not involved at all spiritually. And we find we are caught in the middle, trying to be with him, to make him comfortable and yet wanting to fully participate in the worship and fellowship.

So the loneliness and sense of separation well up once again.

*What type of loneliness troubles us?* Dr. David Claerbaut, psychologist, sociologist, and professor, in his book *Liberation from Loneliness* emphasizes, "Loneliness is common. Everyone experiences it." He goes on to say, "It can't be avoided, but it can be overcome."[1]

In *Loneliness Is Not a Disease,* Tim Timmons writes, "Loneliness is an unhappy combination of anxiety and insecurity, fear of rejection and failure, a deep sense of loss and isolation. . . ."[2]

The kind of loneliness we experience at church stems from realities beyond our control, such as our husbands' lack of faith and the fact that most people attend church and church activities with their spouses. These circumstances trigger situations where we feel different, odd, isolated.

*Don't take it personally.* If we struggle with low self-esteem—and most of us do, at least at times—we may assume when we feel overlooked and lonely that it is because we are unlovable. We need to understand that we have not been ignored because people don't like us. Rather, our feelings of isolation are caused by the circumstances.

We must not jump to conclusions or read too much into events that may seem like rejection to us. The empty chair left next to us is probably just a reflection of our human tendency to allow each other plenty of space. Other rebuffs are certainly thoughtless, but most often they are not aimed at us personally.

Still the loneliness is painful and makes us want to run from our feelings. If we stop to look at them, to really feel them, we fear they might drown us or we could lose control. Just the opposite is true. We have a much better chance of finding ways of overcoming our loneliness not by denying it but by stopping to feel, understand, and accept our feelings. We are not talking here about wallowing in self-pity—that is never healthy—but rather we need to make an honest appraisal of things as they really are.

*How about some answers?* Now what? All the women we talked with agreed that if they dwelt on their feelings and did nothing they simply felt sorry for themselves and compounded their loneliness.

What, then, are the answers to this downward spiral? Our ideal solution—that our husbands become Christians or get excited about church—is out, at least for now. We can't make it happen. If we could, we would have done it long ago. So we need to find some things we can do to minimize the loneliness.

First, don't leave an empty chair. On those occasions when you do step alone into a worship service or church function, do you leave an empty chair next to you when you sit down? Go ahead! Be brave. Sit next to a stranger. Introduce yourself. If you take the initiative in greeting them, they will know you would like to know them, and you may just make a new acquaintance.

Although not everyone we sit beside will want to talk, we have met some wonderful people just this way. We particularly look for another woman alone and find she often welcomes our company.

Another very practical way to forestall much of the loneliness is to plan to go with someone or to meet another person at church or a church function. All of us know a woman who comes alone to church, whether it is a young single, an elderly widow, or a woman who is separated from her husband. Chances are, she is feeling uncomfortable, too. You would do both of you a favor if you offered to pick her up or to meet her. Perhaps this might be a burden on a regular basis, but try it occasionally. If you can't think of anyone to invite, call the church office and offer to bring someone who needs a ride.

And next time there is a dinner or party scheduled, why not plan a table? You might make up a "ladies' table," including widows and singles, as well as the spiritually single.

This can be fun and satisfying when you plan it yourselves, whereas some women might feel ostracized if it is set up by your church leadership. On the other hand, your table doesn't necessarily have to be all singles. Try mixing couples and women who are alone. Everyone loves to be wanted, to be asked.

One woman bought all the tickets for a table at a Christmas banquet and asked people to sit with her, promising that one of the party would go early to save the table. "They loved knowing seats would be saved for them," she recalls.

You can also try women's ministries. You may find that you are more comfortable if you concentrate your involvement at church upon women's activities that husbands do not attend. And becoming a part of a small group can help you get acquainted and feel less alone. (It also broadens the number of people who recognize you and whom you know at Sunday services.) A Bible study, support group, or an outreach ministry in the community are just a few of the activities that will give you the feeling of spiritual family.

However, we both try to choose activities that don't take us away too often when our husbands are home.

Above all, focus on the Lord. The most important cure for loneliness due to circumstances, however, is to take your eyes off yourself and focus on the Lord. When you feel alone in church, think about why you are there—to worship the Lord. Turn your eyes on Jesus and praise him! Tell him how much you love him and close your eyes to your surroundings. When you meditate on God's gracious, unconditional love—his countless benefits, how can you possibly feel lonely?

One young mother, who confessed "lots of tears over loneliness," told how she turned to God and he spoke to her heart: "Am I not enough for you, child? Rest in me. Allow me to fill your needs and comfort your heart." When she chose to obey, she reports, "I was never lonely again in any circumstance of life."

Isn't that exactly what God promises us? "Never will I

leave you. Never will I forsake you," he said (Heb. 13:5b). And remember how Jesus assured us, "Surely I am with you always, even to the end of the earth"? (Matt. 28:20b).

The Book of Isaiah overflows with promises that God will not forsake or forget us, such as "'Though the mountains be shaken and the hills be removed, yet my unfailing love for you will not be shaken nor my covenant of peace be removed,' says the Lord who has compassion on you" (Isa. 54:10).

And best of all, God has promised us that nothing can separate us from his love—not even death or life, angels or demons (Rom. 8:35-39). What a reassurance to a lonely wife!

## LONELINESS AT HOME

Loneliness means also not being able to share with our husbands. Loneliness in church is one thing, but often the most acute sense of aloneness arises at home. As women, we have a deep need for intimacy, but here is a vital dimension of our lives in which we cannot be intimate with our husbands. "My walk with the Lord is absolutely the most important facet of my life. But I can't share it with the most important person in my life, my husband," lamented Judy.

Nancy, whose husband later became a believer, recalls earlier days when "I'd come home from the most glorious worship services, so filled with joy. And I would stand outside the front door and literally psyche myself down before going inside. There was no way I could express the depth of my feelings, the excitement of what I'd learned, to my husband."

*Marriage was supposed to resolve loneliness.* Most of us expected that marriage would be the end of loneliness for us. We thought husbands and wives were to be best friends, or as Scripture says, "one flesh." Now because of our spiritual differences, we find we are still lonely—sometimes desperately lonely.

15

In his book, *Liberation from Loneliness,* Dr. Claerbaut explains, "One of the great illusions of our age is that simply having a relationship—any relationship, whether romantic or friendly—will combat loneliness. In reality, unfulfilling relationships often intensify loneliness."[3]

Because we expected our marriage to keep us from being lonely and it hasn't, we feel cheated. And when our husbands are totally unaware of our loneliness, that is even more infuriating.

Have you ever caught yourself thinking thoughts like this: "If my husband would just become a committed Christian like me, then we could share and I wouldn't be lonely anymore"? It sounds wonderful, but it is not realistic, perhaps not even mature!

Our loneliness is not the direct result of the fact that our husband is not an active Christian. Rather, the feelings come from how we respond to that fact. Our feelings are the result of the way we talk to ourselves inside about his lack of faith.

We become more lonely when we tell ourselves over and over how painful it is to be married to someone who doesn't share our commitment to the Lord, dwelling on how much we miss it and how terrible it is for the children. But when we remind ourselves of the positive things in our marriage, of the good things we have, the feelings of loneliness will diminish.

We must learn to accept responsibility for our own feelings. Only then can we begin to do something about them. Dr. Archibald Hart, professor of psychology at Fuller Theological Seminary in Pasadena, says in his book *Feeling Free,* "If we control our self-talk and begin to think and talk more rationally and objectively, we can do a turnabout in our emotions."[4]

*Don't withdraw emotionally.* Another way we can reduce the loneliness in our relationship with our husbands is by continuing to share feelings. Too many times we stop sharing because of the negative response we get from our husbands. Have you ever discovered a new spiritual truth in a Bible study and tried to share it with your husband? Did you get a blank look that made you feel like he thought you had just come from outer space? Perhaps he made some sarcastic remark, or he may have been irritated, even angry. If you are like us, after a while, you gave up sharing things about church. It was too painful. And you may have stopped sharing a lot of other things you feel deeply about, too.

But that is a mistake. It causes separation and of course, loneliness. There is an essential part of us that we now keep tucked away from our husbands. Instead, we need to keep sharing from all areas of our lives. And when it comes to the spiritual, we can emphasize not what happened, but how we feel about what happened. Share spontaneously, telling what you are excited about, just as easily and naturally as you might tell of taking the kids to the zoo.

Our purpose is not to convert our husbands or to please them. In fact, we need to allow them to respond in any way they will. Our purpose is simply to be open with them, to let them know us.

As we open up our feelings to our husbands, they may eventually feel safe enough to share their feelings in return. Even if our husbands react negatively, we will get to know them better. And our loneliness will diminish.

Diane told us that she has shared almost everything about her life at church with her unbelieving husband for the twenty-nine years of their marriage. "I didn't just tell him the good stuff. I also told him when I was disappointed or upset."

"Didn't he ever get angry or irritated with your sharing?" we asked.

"Of course," she replied. "But he is supposed to be my comforter, to care about me. Even when he failed to do this, it was his responsibility. He couldn't respond if he didn't know how I felt, so I just kept on sharing. Now he has received the Lord and we have a wonderful, close marriage."

Both of us find sharing our feelings about our faith with our husbands very difficult. But now, because of what we have learned in researching this book and in talking to women who have kept openly sharing with their husbands, we feel challenged to try. We are still beginners at it, but so far we like the warmth we have experienced.

If you have a husband who explodes to keep you from sharing anything related to your Christianity, you may need to start with sharing your feelings in bits and pieces, beginning with safer subjects. Be wise, and ask God to guide you, but share with your husband as much as you can of the real you—of how you feel deep inside.

*We need intimacy (but men may not).* We need to be aware of something else. Most men do not feel a great need for intimacy, while women crave it. Because men are basically competitive, they may, in fact, view intimacy as a sign of weakness. They may fear that letting others (even us) know their innermost feelings gives others power over them. Further, in *Sex Roles and the Christian Family,* Peter Blitchington reminds us that men are more task oriented and tend to focus on accomplishments rather than on relationships, so intimacy is not a priority with them.[5]

Psychologist Carol Gilligan, who explored male-female differences in her book, *In a Different Voice,* theorizes that men seek autonomy and are threatened by intimacy, while women seek connectedness and are threatened by isolation.[6]

This is why it is rare for a woman, even with a Christian husband, to be able to satisfy her need for intimate communication with her husband alone. It takes some of us a long time to realize this.

As children, we may have found our mothers' warm relationships with other women "just too icky sweet." Or we wondered how our mothers at the Women's Mission Society ever managed to sew any layettes for the missionaries or roll any bandages for the leper colony, with all the talking that went on. Now, however, we begin to understand how much women need each other to talk about their feelings, their struggles, and their joys.

While this is true for most women, it is much more urgent for wives of unbelieving or lukewarm Christian husbands. It is vital that we find other Christian women with whom we can share the things of the Lord, in a telephone conversation or through a Bible study, a prayer group, a women's luncheon. It is essential that we encourage one another, pray for one another, and hold ourselves accountable to one another. It is especially helpful if we can find a few women who have situations similar to ours.

## OUR ULTIMATE, INTIMATE FRIEND

One wife told us her marriage was headed for divorce because "I wanted my husband and me to share everything in a highly intimate, communicative relationship. When he wouldn't, I felt so lonely. I thought I had married the wrong man. Finally I realized that God alone is the one with whom we can be totally and continually intimate. Only then could I see all the many strong points of my introverted scientist husband, and stop asking the impossible of him."

Did you know that there are many biblical references to the Lord as a husband? Isaiah wrote to widows, "For your Maker is your husband—the Lord Almighty is his name— the Holy One of Israel is your Redeemer; he is called the God of all the earth" (Isa. 54:5).

If God promises to be a husband to the widowed, we think we can ask him to fill in for our husbands in the areas where they are not yet able to fulfill their responsibilities as Christian husbands.

Notice, too, that Jesus calls us his friends! ( John 15:13–16). How we praise him for that precious relationship which allows us to tell him the deepest thoughts of our hearts and to know that he understands in a way that no one else can achieve! Remember, Jesus must have felt terribly lonely at times here on earth. His disciples—those closest to him—

19

didn't understand him. Gethsemane and the crucifixion must have been devastatingly lonely experiences.

We shouldn't demand the impossible of our husbands—that they meet all our needs for intimacy. But we can ask "the impossible" of God. It is so important to be honest with him! Tell him about your loneliness. Jesus pointed out that he did not come to help those whose lives were "perfect," but those who were ill (Mark 2:17). God can help only those who admit they have a problem.

Tell him about it. He knows how it feels.

## QUESTIONS FOR FURTHER STUDY
## AND GROUP DISCUSSION

This section of each chapter is designed to be used in a small discussion group. Each member should read the chapter and answer the questions before you meet. Then when you come together, discuss your answers.

At your first group meeting, take time to get acquainted. Introduce yourselves and share a bit about your husbands and families. To make your group a safe place to be open and honest, be sure to keep confidential all that is shared.

1. Going to church alone is difficult for many of us. Why is it important to attend church? What may happen to our Christian life if we do not have fellowship? Where and when do you fellowship with the body of Christ?

Read *Hebrews 10:23-25*.

2. What causes you the most loneliness at church or church activities? What helps you to avoid such feelings or to deal with them successfully? Discuss with your group some ways you might help each other to minimize the loneliness.

3. Make a list of excellent qualities and attributes of God that you can use to praise him rather than focusing on your loneliness. Here are some verses to get you started:

20

4/28 Homework for 3/5

*Numbers 23:19*
*Matthew 28:20b*
*Romans 5:6-8; 8:1, 28, 38-39*
*Philippians 1:6*
*Hebrews 1:3; 13:5b, 8*
*1 John 4:19*
*Jude 24*

Share your list with your group. Have you used it in worship? Did it help you focus on the Lord?

4/28

(4.) Another way we can focus on the Lord is to imagine ourselves with him in a scriptural picture. For example, we could be walking in a meadow with the Good Shepherd of Psalm 23 or kneeling before the throne of Revelation 1. From the following passages and others you remember, make a note of your favorites for your wallet or Bible, so you can pull them out next time you wish to focus on him.

*Exodus 19:9, 16-21*
*Psalm 23*
*Matthew 3:13-17*
*Matthew 19:13-15*
*Mark 4:1-2*
*Mark 14:3-9*
*Mark 15:12-41*
*Revelation 1:12-18*

Tell your group about your worship experiences. What pictures did you use? In what ways did picturing the Lord make worship easier? How long did you keep the picture in your mind? Did you use more than one picture?

5. Do you ever feel lonely in your marriage? Do you share your feelings with your husband without expecting a specific response from him? Does he share his feelings with you? Why or why not? Relate an example of sharing your feelings with your husband to your group. Then talk about

what keeps people from sharing feelings. Why might a husband resist sharing?

6. Do you have women friends in whom you can confide intimately? Does that make you feel less lonely? How have you developed such relationships? What do you do to maintain such friendships?

7. Read *John 15:13-15*. How does Jesus become our friend? How is your life different with Jesus as your friend? Ask the Holy Spirit to show you how to make this truth come alive for you. Share any new ideas from the Holy Spirit with your group.

8. Read *Isaiah 54:1-8* and *2 Corinthians 11:2*. In what ways is the Lord your spiritual husband? What needs does he meet for you that your husband cannot or does not? Although your answers to this question may be very personal, share what you can with the group. It will help others to reach for all God has for them.

**Close your discussion with a time of prayer for each other's needs and for all your husbands.**

# TWO
# THOSE GREAT EXPECTATIONS

"Someday," we tell ourselves, as we drift off on the pink cloud of our fondest dreams, "everything will change. My husband will wholeheartedly commit himself to the Lord, and he will become Mr. Wonderful. (After all, he will be a new person in Christ.) He will never again be short-tempered, sloppy, self-centered, impatient, or complain that there are three unmatched socks in his drawer.

"When we are both totally committed to the Lord, my husband and I will be best friends. I will be able to confide my most special thoughts to him and we will talk easily about everything. We will always be considerate of each other. We will always pray together for God's guidance. And we will have exactly the same goals and look at things from the same perspective. So of course, we will come to perfect agreement on everything. Why, we will walk off into the sunset, hand in hand, and live happily ever after!"

What a wonderful dream! Yet it is never-never land, just as real as frogs that turn into princes and knights in shining armor who sweep girls away on white horses, leaving all of life's problems behind.

But as we dream and hope and wait . . . and wait . . . for our husbands to receive the gift of faith or to finally get fired up about God, we do tend to develop highly idealized expectations.


## WHERE DO WE GET THESE IDEAS?

While some of our hopes and dreams stem from our own imaginative wishful thinking, we also get a lot of help from the world around us.

*Some dreams spring from the testimonies of others.* We begin to form ideas of what a marriage can be when we listen to exceptional testimonies. "My husband squandered all our savings in Las Vegas and he came home drunk almost every night, but now that he knows the Lord, all that's changed completely."

After hearing such a testimony, we visualize our husband's most annoying habits gone forever. Perhaps for you it is his swearing, his explosive temper, or how about his messy garage?

Or possibly you hear another wife testify, "George was a workaholic. He was never home in time for dinner with the children, and because he would go into work on Saturday and bring his briefcase home to work on Sunday, we never did anything as a family. But when he accepted the Lord, he did a 180-degree turnaround. Now he takes me out to dinner once a week. He spends time with the family almost every evening, and he has become involved in helping with our son's Sunday school class."

Now you see your husband becoming considerate, thoughtful, so sensitive and caring toward you and the children! The last time he brought you flowers was when you were dating, but now you can almost smell the roses he will bring for Valentine's Day! And no longer will he come home and plop down in front of the TV. He will look forward to spending time with the children, teaching Johnny to play ball, and helping Susie ride her bike.

Even more difficult for the wife of an unbelieving husband are testimonies of joint prayer and oneness in the Lord.

"Our son was on drugs, dropped out of school, and was absolutely beyond our control. Jeff and I just stood fast together in prayer and believed that the Lord would deliver our boy. I can't tell you what it meant to be so united in trust and faith! It took two years, but today our son is clean and back in college and doing just wonderfully."

Again your imagination runs away. Can't you just see yourself telling your husband how concerned you are over Sammy's grades, and then both of you kneeling together by your bed to pray for him? Or maybe your daughter and her boyfriend have had a fight. When you tell your husband, he calls Diane in for a loving talk and then you all join hands in prayer.

Because we are so hungry for change in our marriage, we make these great imaginative leaps, assuming or presuming that what happened to one couple can be transferred to our situation. After all, God is no respecter of persons, right?

That is true, but he has made each of us unique. And because your husband is different from any other man, God will deal with him in the way that is best for him, not necessarily as he dealt with Sally's or Marcy's husbands. Your husband's response will not be quite like their husbands' either. Change will come only when he is ready.

*Other expectations come from teaching in church.* A great deal of teaching in our churches on marriage also feeds our fantasies. We go filled with hope that we will glean something that will enrich our marriages. But the speaker usually assumes that both spouses are Christians, attending church, and willing to change in order to do things God's way. The teachings often lift up someone's idea of the ideal marriage, feeding our hunger for change, and multiplying our frustration when we realize how helpless we are to make those changes. The hurts and disappointments that come almost daily with being married to unbelieving or barely believing husbands are practically never dealt with.

One woman who attended a marriage seminar told us, "I cried all the way home. They sure don't live at my house.

They have no idea what I deal with. I went for help, but now I feel so hopeless! I desperately want the kind of marriage they talk about, but I can't make it happen."

Another major problem is that much of the teaching is given by men, so it usually emphasizes the things that husbands should do. It is easy to assume that when a Christian husband hears such teaching he also successfully incorporates it into his marriage. And we can hardly wait till our husband is a believer who does all these things, too.

We fail to understand that these teachings on marriage are stressed over and over again in the church because most men, even Christian men, find them difficult to assimilate and put into practice. Women are generally eager to improve their marriages, but men often feel no need to change. They may have little hunger for such closeness as praying together, times of communication, romance. That is why these matters must be taught—and learned. We hear about them because so few men do them well.

*We are caught up in the "greener grass" syndrome.* When we look at Christian couples interacting within the church, smiling, and listening attentively to one another, holding hands, we may believe that they relate this way all the time. We never hear him speak a sharp word to her. And he is so gracious, so warm to everyone at church that we assume he is equally agreeable at home. Rarely do these couples share any problems they may have within their Christian homes, so we assume, of course, that they haven't any.

We forget that most of us put on our good Christian masks at church. ("How are you?" "Just wonderful!") After all, who deliberately parades dirty laundry in public? It is usually only in small, safe groups that Christians begin to open up and share some of the hurts and hard places in their marriages.

We fail to realize that, as psychologist Michele McCormick points out, "All marriages have rough spots."

Dr. McCormick, of CORE, a Christian counseling center in Newport Beach, California, adds, "Marriage is not easy. Most suffer in the area of communication and intimacy."

For a graduate research project, Dr. McCormick surveyed the Christian faculty of her university and was "shocked" at the lack of intimacy in marriage that was revealed. "Because of the fall, because of our nature, we all have to work at marriage," she emphasizes.

*You expected maybe Billy Graham?* If your husband considers himself a Christian, do you question his commitment because he doesn't meet your expectations? When you look at the great leaders of our time, perhaps you feel your husband should perform with equal effectiveness. If he really believes, why doesn't he proclaim his faith wherever he goes, step forward to participate in Sunday services, or at least start a Bible study at work, or witness to the neighbors next door?

But think a moment. Is that his God-given nature? If he is quiet and unassuming, is it logical to expect him suddenly to develop an overactive thyroid or Type A personality? No matter how firm his Christian foundation, these traits may never develop.

"I finally learned that still waters can run very deep," Rhonda told us. "Absolutely the dumbest thing I can do for a low-key guy like my husband is to push or pressure or, worst of all—tell him all the things he isn't."

Perhaps your husband is one who will provide background support, be an intercessor in prayer, make his home available for a study group, or be a friend and encourager to just one person. Back off, pray, and give him a chance to find his own place in the body of Christ.

*Books also may fuel our anticipation.* In our eagerness to help our husbands, often we turn to books and articles in search of answers. Some imply that we are God's special agents, commissioned to reach our unsaved husbands, and that we must be ever mindful of this awesome responsibility. What a heavy burden!

Yet we are hungry for help, so when we find a specific

"technique" to use, our hopes may rise once again. If we follow a certain prescribed set of behavior, we are told, we will surely execute a spiritual squeeze play that will bring our mate to his knees before the Lord. Sometimes sample dialogue is even scripted out for us. If only such a claim were true!

The books offer us all kinds of advice, from telling him of our faith to not saying a word; from refusing to be unequally yoked to becoming totally submissive to him. We try, oh, so hard, but he hardly notices. Eventually we become exhausted, and we feel like a failure as a Christian, as though his lack of response is all our fault. We forget we do not have the power to change our husbands.

*Sometimes our husbands raise our hopes.* Just when we think our husbands will never show any interest in the Lord, they may surprise us. For example, a spouse may agree to go to that special Thanksgiving or Christmas or Easter service with you. Or he might even decide to join you at a Bible study, a seminar, or a Billy Graham crusade. Part of you knows he is doing it to please you, because he knows it is important to you. But part of you says, "Oh, maybe this will be the time!"

How pleased you are to have him at your side! But you are so busy praying for him, so concerned with his reactions, you scarcely hear the speaker. If your husband repeatedly looks at his watch or makes a running commentary on the service or sermon, it is impossible for you to focus on the Lord. Then perhaps there is an invitation to receive Christ. Oh, how you pray!

And nothing happens. Afterward, he may be silent. Or he may attack what was said. Or he may agree that the speaker was good, but "I don't need what he's selling."

Sometimes we feel certain that we are seeing progress. Janet felt elated and encouraged when her husband began attending church regularly with her. He even built some bulletin boards for Sunday school. Surely he was "getting close." Then, for two successive Sundays he was "too busy at work" to go to church. The following week he announced his plans to travel to a national meeting of a cult that emphasizes Hindu mysticism, and Janet's hopes crashed.

Or our husbands may develop a friendship with a Christian neighbor or coworker. And we think surely that this is the one God has sent to lead our husbands to him. Then the neighbor moves or the coworker is transferred, and we are back to square one.

Or are we? Even though we see no progress through these experiences, seeds may have been planted in our husbands' lives. And when our ideas seem to fail, we come right back where we belong—trusting God, knowing he alone can effect change.

*Times of tragedy may raise our hopes, too.* Early in our Christian experience, we both prayed, "Oh, Lord, draw my husband to you, but don't make it too hard or painful for him (or me)."

As the years went by, we each came to a point of rest, knowing that God has his own way to draw each person to him and, whatever it is, it will be exactly right.

But occasionally, some small part of us has wondered if something awful, perhaps some tragedy, must occur to bring our husbands to the Lord.

Many people in the "world" believe that it is people in desperation who become Christians. They think people turn to God because they need a crutch. One unbelieving husband explained it this way: "They say there are no atheists in foxholes. So, I guess I just haven't been in a deep enough foxhole yet."

Pam's mother-in-law expressed this same belief, common to many Christians. She confided to Pam, "Well, I hate to say it, but it will probably take something really devastating to bring my son to his knees. I'm praying that God will do whatever is necessary, no matter what the cost, to open his eyes to the truth."

Christian friends may even suggest this. And we have

heard some well-meaning Christians actually pray for a crisis to "open his eyes to the truth." Then, when times of crisis do arise, we tend to expect something to happen.

Karen had been married to an unbelieving husband for thirty-five years. When he suffered a heart attack, she was certain that this graphic demonstration of his mortality would trigger in him a new interest in the Lord. But when she tried to broach the subject, he refused to discuss it. In her deep concern, she cried, "Dave, I have a right to know where you are spiritually!" Still he would not reply, and Karen was left frustrated, angry, and worried!

It is true, of course, that when a man reaches the end of his own resources, he may turn to God. And these are the testimonies we hear most often, because they are so dramatic. But as the song says, "It ain't necessarily so." And we would add, "It ain't necessarily necessary."

Neither of us came to the Lord through tragedy. Our husbands' time of conversion may not be at all what we anticipate. It may come when one or the other finds his job not fulfilling, or when he picks up a Gideon Bible in a hotel on a business trip, or simply when all that he has heard through the years meshes together and that moment comes when he can say, "I believe!"

*Expectations of others sometimes corner us.* When the women (and men) with whom we fellowship ask, "How's that husband of yours doing?" usually it comes through to us as a caring inquiry, an expression of hang-in-there-baby support. But sometimes the tone of voice subtly transforms it to a demand for a progress report. The implication seems to be, "Hasn't he made any headway yet? Are you handling this right? Surely by now. . . ." Sometimes we also hear magic solutions, such as, "If you could just get him into a Bible study fellowship. . . ."

It is difficult, but we try not to let others lay their expectations or a sense of responsibility on us. Here are responses we sometimes use: "He'll come in God's time," or "God knows what the problems are and I trust him," or

"Thanks for your concern; I'd really appreciate your prayers."

## TOWARD MORE REALISTIC EXPECTATIONS

How can we release some of the unreal expectations we have created or assimilated through the years? If we can develop more realistic expectations for our marriage, we won't experience so many disappointments or become so discouraged over the slowness of our husband's salvation or his Christian growth.

In Proverbs 13:12 we read, "Hope deferred makes the heart sick; but a longing fulfilled is a tree of life." We need dreams that have the potential of coming true, not those that are beyond God's will for us.

So what are realistic expectations for a Christian wife? Let us go back to creation.

## MARRIAGE IS COMPLEMENTARY ONENESS

After God made woman and brought her to her husband, Adam exclaimed, "This is now bone of my bones and flesh of my flesh; she shall be called 'woman' for she was taken out of man" (Gen. 2:23-24). The passage continues, "For this reason a man will leave his father and mother and be united to his wife, and they will become one flesh."

Too often we think that becoming "one" means we will become alike, that there will be no differences. We will have the same likes and dislikes, the same aspirations. Then when this doesn't happen in our marriage, we feel crushed, cheated.

But God never intended that a husband and wife be photocopies of each other. Elisabeth Elliot, in her book, *The Mark of a Man*, catches a bit of the brilliance of God's plan. She describes man and woman as "two creatures amazingly alike and wonderfully different."[1]

God has purposely built us with differences that complement one another. Yet, like a key and a lock, we fit together to make a working, interdependent, interconnected whole— or as the Bible puts it, "one flesh" (Gen. 2:24).

These complementary differences in us are planned by God for our good, yet they do not always make us comfortable with each other. In fact, sometimes we find them quite abrasive. But we believe this too is part of God's plan. He intends that we pull and push a little at each other within our marriage. It stretches us, makes us grow. It builds character and is one way God uses to gently mold us into the image of Jesus. (Uh-oh! There go our dreams of perfect harmony in marriage!)

## SO WHAT ARE THE DIFFERENCES BETWEEN MEN AND WOMEN?

In Genesis we read, "So God created man in his own image . . . male and female he created them" (1:27). Notice those masculine-feminine differences God created in us.

Of course we know we are physically different. But because in recent years our society has emphasized the similarities in the sexes and minimized the dissimilarities, many of us have lost awareness of the subtle variations. Then, unrealistically, we often expect our husbands to act and respond as we would—in a feminine manner—and our husbands no doubt sometimes complain, like Professor Higgins in *My Fair Lady,* "Why can't a woman be more like a man?"

Before we examine the basic differences, we need to understand that we all have both masculine and feminine characteristics. In a group of a hundred men and a hundred women, there would be some men with a number of feminine attributes and some women with many male qualities. However, if we tested all two hundred people, the differences between the sexes would be statistically demonstrable.

As we look at the sex contrasts, keep in mind we are dealing with generalities and that individuals vary greatly.

God made men generally taller, heavier, and physically stronger than women. They have longer legs and longer arms—both distinct advantages in a physical fight. God gave them an aggressive, dominant nature so they could lead, protect, and provide for their families.[2] Research clearly confirms this male aggressiveness and shows it to be related to the male hormone, testosterone.[3]

Boys tend to do better in the mathematical, mechanical areas of standardized intelligence tests while scoring lower than girls in the verbal areas.

Getting something done, accomplishing a goal, may be more important to men [4] than personal relationships or feelings—either their own or others'. In fact, they often are not in touch with their own feelings, nor are they very aware of the feelings of others. Psychologist Lillian Rubin, after researching men and women's friendships, says, "It's not that men don't think it matters; it's that that stuff, that inner, interior stuff, is not accessible to them. They don't know how to go in there."[5] Men marry women who are more feminine than they. Further, they look for a woman who needs them, whom they can take care of. They also want someone who is gentler, kinder, a little more moral than they. They may ridicule a woman's ideals just to see if she sticks by what she says, but they lose respect for her if they can knock her off her pedestal.

When competing with women, they have a strong need to win in what they consider male activities, such as sports and mechanical pursuits. This need to win over women pushes them to strive for headship in their home. And they are so humiliated by losing, they may refuse to compete with their wives in areas where the woman might win. Dr. Joyce Brothers, in her book *What Every Woman Should Know About Men*, says, "What women should know about men is that they do not mind working with women—as long as they are the boss."[6]

Because a man must compete out in the world to provide

for his family, he may consider his wife the only safe person in his life, his only real friend. Friendship to men is usually not having or being a confidante, with intimate sharing of feelings and dreams, but a bottom line, "I'll be there for you" relationship.

God made women with a smaller frame, larger hips (to accommodate pregnancy), and more fat cells that give their bodies those delightful, soft curves men like so much. Our skin is thinner, which makes it softer to touch, but unfortunately allows it to wrinkle sooner than the thicker skin of men.

Women tend to excel in the verbal parts of intelligence tests. That means they usually talk more easily. And they tend to spend more time reading and usually enjoy it more than their husbands.

Women are nuturant—relationship-oriented.[7] We care about people and are sensitive to our feelings and those of others. Because we are more observant of and respond to facial expressions and body language that express feelings, we sometimes seem illogical to men. Our priorities center around relationships and people rather than tasks and goals.[8] As nurturers, women work to help their children, their husbands, and others to grow, often sacrificing their own desires for what is best for others.

Women tend to marry men who are more masculine than themselves. God told Eve that her desire would be for her husband (Gen. 3:16), and most women today still desire the security a husband and marriage can provide. Women are nest builders, wanting a home and steady income, so they can raise their children in safety.

Yet women are also generally more able to adapt or change when necessary. Because they are not as competitive and aggressive as men, they usually have more patience and are willing to compromise.[9] This allows them to adjust to the needs and headship of their own husbands. Because women love warm, intimate relationships where feelings are shared, they may feel rejected when their husbands are unwilling or unable to connect with them on this level. Recognizing that many husbands do not relate intimately with their wives, Dr. James Dobson in his film series, *Focus on the Family,* points out that women need friendships with other women to meet this need.

Since God made us in such infinite variety, we see areas in most marriages where the wife or husband crosses over to a characteristic of the opposite sex. Jan's husband is very sensitive to feelings, while Jan is often more logical, responding to external circumstances. Sue is exceptionally skilled in math, so she keeps the budget and checkbook in her family. Jim's hobby is gourmet cooking, so he often cooks Sunday dinner.

Crossovers that work for both you and your husband are great. But your marriage may be headed for trouble if you compete with your husband in areas he considers masculine or within his realm of expertise. If you are even moderately successful, he may feel diminished as a man.

## HAVE YOU EXPECTED YOUR HUSBAND TO REACT LIKE A WOMAN?

Unknowingly, many of us have expected our husbands to respond in feminine ways. Pat spent years thinking that her husband was, at times, stubborn and selfish because he wasn't as patient, kind, and tender as she felt he should be. Actually, he was simply being masculine, while she looked for feminine responses.

Such expectations can also be a trap for the wife of the foot-dragging Christian, who may feel that if her husband were really rooted and grounded in his faith, he would talk openly and in depth about his spiritual walk and spend more time reading Christian books. Anne Ortlund, author of *Building a Great Marriage* and *Disciplines of the Beautiful Woman,* observed that many wives assume that their husbands are "less spiritual" when this isn't the case. As we have seen, men may not be as verbal as women, and they may not like to read extensively. They also may not have as much available time to spend in the Word.

Are you beginning to see how important it is to understand clearly the male–female differences? God created them within us, so it's important to adjust our expectations to harmonize with our husbands' masculinity.

It helps us see, for instance, that although our husbands can learn to open up and share more, they will probably never hunger for that kind of intimacy, nor will they enjoy it as much as we. They can also learn to be more sensitive to our feelings, to meet our needs for romantic love, but it does not come naturally to them to be sentimental or tender. And even though they may enjoy a nice home, it is not likely to be as important to them as it is to us.

## DO YOU EXPECT YOUR HUSBAND TO MEET ALL YOUR NEEDS?

Some of us have yet another area of unreasonable expectations that can be devastating to our marriage. As a newlywed, Bev held fast to the fairy-tale expectation that her husband would be the primary meeter of her needs: her need for love, friendship, encouragement, understanding, security, and much more. To her great surprise, he wasn't. She felt unloved, rejected—and angry. Only when she came to the Lord did she realize the impossible demands she had silently placed upon her husband—needs that could be met only by God, who, indeed, promises to supply all our needs. She feels that without God, her marriage could not have survived.

No human being, no matter how wonderful, can meet all our needs. If they could, we would never reach out to God. He planned that we would feel a bit empty, insecure, incomplete without him, that people would never be enough. He is the only one who can fill the void.

## WOMEN WHOSE HUSBANDS BECAME BELIEVERS

To gain a more realistic perspective on how life can change we interviewed a number of women who, after many years of waiting and praying, saw their husbands become believers.

Sharon laughingly admitted that her husband did not become a different person. "I used to feel frustrated because he spent so much time out with the guys. Now he is so involved in the church, he's gone just as much as he ever was. And no, we don't have a perfect spiritual sharing, because he hasn't the time to spend in Bible study that I do. Often, I'll bring up some new insight which has absolutely thrilled me, and he'll say, 'Uh huh,' and that's the end of that!"

Another wife referred to the "uncomfortableness" she felt after her husband received the Lord. "Before, there had been a lot of predictability. I pretty much knew what his reactions would be. Now, especially during this time of transition, I don't know what to expect of him. Some things have changed and some have not. I'm never sure. We communicate more, yes. But we also experience more disagreements—probably because we're talking and spending a lot more time together. We have different backgrounds, so we still view many things differently."

She added that since they now go to many church functions together, she has had to reduce her women's activities, which has affected her ability to fellowship with her friends. Even though there are more frustrations than she expected, she is more than thrilled that her husband has come to Christ.

Kerry also found "a whole new ball game, because the old guidelines are gone. The question is, what is my place now? What do I keep on doing and what do I not do? What behavior in him will stay and what will change?"

She found too that her husband's old habits didn't magically change. "It was very gradual, over more than ten years. For many years, he had been physically abusive, and it took time for him to learn how to handle his anger. But one day he actually told me, 'I can never be nice enough to make it up to you.' But of course he's not perfect—yet."

Kerry added, "He's always seen me as the 'spiritual one,' and for a long time I sensed a little anger or perhaps envy, because he was the babe and I was the more mature believer, although I was very careful not to be self-righteous or parade what I know in front of him. When the Lord told me I had to apologize to my husband for making him uncomfortable, it was the hardest thing I've ever done because I felt I hadn't done anything wrong. Yet I was obedient. And he wept when I told him I was there to be his helper, to serve him. I think we have to realize that both before and after they are saved, we are not our husbands' teachers."

Although there may be specific areas of spectacular change in some husbands when they receive Christ or make a total commitment of their lives to the Lord, several wives mentioned how very slow their husbands' growth in the Lord appeared to be. "I forget," confessed Janie, "that I wasn't an overnight miracle. I guess I thought he'd be more gung-ho, more thirsty to learn than he is. He's moving very cautiously and doesn't talk a lot about it yet."

## HOW CAN WE GET RID OF OUR UNREALISTIC EXPECTATIONS?

Expectations are feelings that stem from what we think, what we value. They don't disappear just because we decide they should. Getting rid of them is a process of changing the way we think, of changing our values. It takes time.

For the two of us, an important antidote to the happily-ever-after fantasy has been to join a small group of women, such as a Bible study, prayer or support group that includes women with believing husbands. Ideally, there will be no more than ten women; about five is even better. Here trust, honesty, and openness can be fostered, and, as the women with Christian spouses begin to share, you will gain first hand a much truer picture of what "the Christian marriage" really is.

In his book *No Condemnation,* psychology professor Dr. Bruce Narramore speaks to those who have difficulty modifying their values. They will find, he says, that change "comes over a lengthy period of time as new and healthier ideals are internalized through the intimate interaction of deep friendships or effective therapy."[10]

It seems that we reorder our thinking and values most often as we relate to other people. That is why an intimate prayer group or Bible study can be so effective in changing and rechanneling our feelings.


## GET ON WITH YOUR OWN CHRISTIAN LIFE

Instead of worrying about when your husband will become a Christian or when he will mature in his faith, get on with your own Christian life. That is your responsibility. Every time disappointment over unfulfilled expectations threatens to overwhelm you, seek the Lord. Praise him, not for what you see, but for who he is. He is always worthy of praise. Then pour your heart out to him and listen. We think you will "hear" words of comfort in your heart, and he may tell you what to do next.

Remember through all of this, God is working for our good, tugging us, molding us into the image of his Son. It isn't always comfortable, but as you seek to be obedient to him, you will find being in the center of his will can bring an immense sense of satisfaction. And you will know the security of being a loved child of your loving Father.

Whenever your expectations threaten to focus on your husband, remember the verse: "Find rest, O my soul, in God alone; my hope comes from him. He alone is my rock and my salvation; he is my fortress, I will not be shaken" (Ps. 62:5–6).

## LIVE TODAY; LEAVE THE FUTURE IN GOD'S HANDS

Of course, we never give up hoping and praying for our husbands. But that doesn't mean living with our eyes forever on what we want in the future. We must learn to live in the now!

Begin by accepting your husband just as he is, with all his flaws. God does! Love him unconditionally now—not because of who or what he is or does—but because he is. It may not be easy, but God will help you learn what it is to truly love him with *agape* love, the kind of love that stems not from your own gotta-do-better efforts or your sentimental heart, but from the power of the Holy Spirit within you. Ask him for it, trusting that "if we love one another, God lives in us and his love is made complete in us" (1 John 4:12).

Our expectations of other people—especially our husbands—only set us up for disappointment; most often, they will not be met. Humans are just so—human! However, this doesn't mean God doesn't care about our dreams, but that he wants so much more for us! Paul reminded us that God "is able to do immeasurably more than all we ask or imagine, according to his power that is at work within us" (Eph. 3:20).

May your expectations, and ours, be from and in him!

## QUESTIONS FOR FURTHER STUDY AND GROUP DISCUSSION

1. List some of the expectations you have had for your husband and for your marriage. Be as specific as possible. Share the expectations that are not too personal with your group, and as the others share, add to your list any additional expectations with which you identify.

2. Ask the Holy Spirit to help you become aware of what has fed or helped develop each expectation you listed above.

Consider all the ideas mentioned in the first half of the chapter.

3. Just how biblical are the male/female differences discussed in this chapter? Look up the sample Scriptures below and list the differences they point out. Then add others that come to mind.

| MEN | WOMEN |
|---|---|
| *Genesis 2:18* | *Genesis 3:16b* |
| *Genesis 3:17-19* | *Proverbs 31:10-31* |
| *Numbers 1:2-3* | *Ephesians 5:22* |
| *Ephesians 5:23* | *Ephesians 5:33b* |
| *Ephesians 5:25-28, 33a* | *Titus 2:3-5* |

4. Next, evaluate your expectations. Take each expectation you listed in Question 1 and ask yourself, Is it biblical? Does it violate any of the male/female differences? Am I expecting my husband to meet needs that I should look to God for? Can I adjust this expectation to make it more realistic or should I just get rid of it? You may need to think and pray about some of your expectations before you can answer the questions above, but at least share your beginnings with your group.

Do 5/5 (if time)

5. Look up the verses below and consider: do you live in the present or do you often think, "When I get this problem taken care of, then I will be happy, or relaxed, or able to do what the Lord wants . . . or . . . or"?

> *Proverbs 3:5*
> *Matthew 6:25-34*
> *Philippians 4:6-8*
> *1 Peter 5:7*

List the "problems" keeping you from living in the present. Share a few of them that keep you living in the future instead of the now. Talk about why it is so difficult to release them to the Lord.

6. What specific steps can we take to help us live in the now and to have realistic expectations of our marriages and our husbands? What will help us trust the Lord more in our hard places? Ask the Holy Spirit to show you how to live today.

7. At the end of the chapter we challenged you to learn to love your husband unconditionally, just as he is now, with *agape* love. That is the kind of love God has for us. Look up *agape* in the dictionary or Bible dictionary. Then consider the following Scriptures that speak of *agape* love.

> *Matthew 5:44*
> *Matthew 19:19b*
> *John 15:12*
> *Ephesians 5:2*
> *1 John 4:7-8*
> *1 Corinthians 13*

Does *agape* love depend on how we feel? Or can we love by action even though our feelings are negative? Think of some examples. Ask God to help you love his way. *Agape* love is impossible to sustain without him.

**Pray for each other that you will be able to release your unrealistic expectations, to love your husband, and to trust the Lord.**

# THREE
# YEARNING FOR HIS SALVATION OR SPIRITUAL MATURITY

When Sally's father-in-law lay in the hospital terminally ill, it was Sally who joined hands in prayer with the dying man and her mother-in-law. Sally's husband, Bill, leaned against the wall, helplessly jingling the change in his pocket. "How I longed at that moment for Bill to know the Lord!" Sally recalls.

It seems that no matter how successful we are at bringing our expectations down to a reasonable level, we still have times when we wish intensely that our husbands were already saved. Painful as it is, this yearning is normal. Yet a closer look may help us live with it in more effective ways.

## WHAT IS OUR MOTIVATION?

When we feel overwhelmed, it helps to ask what our motivation is in seeking our husbands' salvation or spiritual maturity.

*Craving for oneness.* Certainly we hunger for a unity in our marriage, a togetherness in our faith. It would be so wonderful to be able to pray together, to read the Word together, and to grow together in the Lord! We would love to present a united front to the children. And to go together to church, or to a Bible study, are dreams we all cherish. We would be so much happier if. . . .

Now isn't that curious? We want to think that we nobly yearn for our husband's salvation for his sake. But suddenly we find ourselves coming back to our own feelings. And there's more.

*It would be so much more convenient.* Let's be honest. It would be much handier for us if our husbands loved the Lord and shared in our priorities as well as our activities. We learned in the last chapter not to have unreasonable expectations, but it does seem we will have fewer problems to cope with when our husbands come to the Lord. Certainly it would be easier to go to church with him than to go alone. And how welcome it would be to enjoy some church activities that we have foregone in the past because we felt we should be home with our husbands, joining in something they chose to do.

Perhaps we need to ask ourselves whether our motivation is to "get him to church" or for his salvation and an intimate relationship with the Lord.

*We will look better.* We know we shouldn't focus on superficial appearances. But we have all felt that certain stigma of being the woman alone at church, the single who isn't really a single. So, of course, we tend to feel we will look better to the rest of the church and to our friends if we have our husbands at our sides in church. "I'm married. Not widowed, not divorced. I want to look like a married woman," Betty admitted.

You may even feel like a second-class Christian because you haven't been able to get your husband to church. Someone may have intimated that there must be something wrong with your Christianity or your husband would have come to the Lord. Certainly many would consider your husband's conversion, when it happens, a testimony of your faith and confirmation of your Christian walk.

It is not so much that you want to look better than others as it is that you feel like an inferior Christian, or fear this is what others think of you.

*We don't want him condemned to hell.* Although some of the earlier reasons for wanting our husband's salvation may seem selfish, this one is literally a matter of life or death for all eternity. We see clearly in the Scriptures that "the wages of sin is death, but the gift of God is eternal life in Christ Jesus our Lord" (Rom. 6:23). We see also, "Whoever believes in the Son has eternal life, but whoever rejects the Son will not see life, for God's wrath remains on him" (John 3:36).

Our heart's desire is for our husbands to receive the gift of eternal life. Because we love them, it is natural for us to long to know that we will someday be in heaven together. Therefore, the possibility of them being separated from us—and God—and being cast into the lake of fire can strike terror into our souls. If we dwell on that, it is no wonder we struggle frantically to try to help along our husband's salvation.

*For God's glory. Vine's Expository Dictionary of Old and New Testament Words* defines *glorify* as "to magnify, extol, praise— ascribe honour to him, acknowledging him as to his being, attributes and acts, i.e., his glory."[1]

If you believe, as we do, that one of our chief purposes in life is to glorify God, then of course you wish for your husband to know the Lord, so he can magnify him. The very act of his coming to the Lord would, of course, testify to God's greatness. For we understand that this will happen not through our own efforts, but through God's grace and mercy.

And then, in our husband's lives, once they know the Lord, we would look forward to the time when their light would shine before men so they may see their good works and glorify our Father (Matt. 5:16).

## WHO IS RESPONSIBLE FOR MY HUSBAND'S SALVATION?

"Is it I, Lord?" Every woman we spoke to told us that at one time or another, she had felt so responsible for her husband's salvation that she did "ridiculous" things to "bring him around," and then felt miserable in her sense of failure when none of them worked.

"I've run the gamut," one wife admitted. "I've left tracts on his pillow, turned on television church services, played Christian programs on the radio. I've planted open books by his chair, put up pertinent Scriptures on the refrigerator or the bathroom mirror. Once, convinced that he would see the light if he would just read C. S. Lewis's *Mere Christianity*, I asked him just to read the fourth chapter while he was on the plane on his next business trip."

Did any of this work?

She shook her head. "He gave me back *Mere Christianity* filled with red penciled comments mirroring his skepticism: 'Dogmatic. Presupposes a finite universe. Maybe yes, maybe no. Author's own definition. Why? Why not?'"

Marcia, on the other hand, decided that the frontal approach of tracts, books, and verses would only antagonize her husband, so she determined to seek his salvation spiritually. She would fast and pray for him every Wednesday until he was saved. Not wanting to call attention to her fast, she decided to skip breakfast and lunch, but to eat dinner with her family.

The first week was wonderful. She felt so spiritual. The next week was almost as good; but about the fifth week she forgot completely about the fasting until noon. Asking the Lord's forgiveness, she fasted on Thursday. The following two weeks she forgot again and had to fast the next day. After the third time, she wondered if maybe, just maybe, this was her idea, not God's. So she asked God to remind her if he wanted her to keep on fasting. When she forgot again, she gave it up. She had to admit that she did not have the spiritual stamina to fight the battle of her husband's salvation without God's help.

Our final resort in trying to expedite our husbands' salvation seems to be nagging. Of course, that isn't what we call it. But we do try to—well, nudge or push a little. And sometimes we manipulate our husbands into exposure to other Christians by getting them together with that nice Christian down the street, or inviting Christians to our homes, or structuring social situations outside the home involving believers.

Of course, we don't fool them for a minute, and sometimes these efforts even backfire. "Don't ever do that to me again!" thundered one unbelieving husband after a dinner party, which was noteworthy to him for its lack of wine or cocktails as well as for round-the-table testimonies of "God's grace in my life."

Why are we surprised at this response? Scripture tells us that no one seeks God (Rom. 3:11). In our lost condition, it is our nature to run from God.

Isn't it time for us to relax and allow God to be God—to know that the battle is not ours, but the Lord's?

Isaiah wrote, "Surely the arm of the Lord is not too short to save" (Isa. 59:1). Believe with us that his hand is indeed long enough and that God is strong enough to save your husband. Yes, even without your help.

## EMOTIONAL OVERLOAD

Sometimes, as we hunger and thirst for our husband's salvation, we feel ourselves going under in a flood of different feelings. What are some of these emotions and how can we handle them?

*That fearful question: "What if . . . ?"* Many women we interviewed spoke of a sometimes overpowering sense of fear. "What if my husband dies tomorrow? Will he go to hell?" they wonder.

"It strikes me hardest each time my husband takes off on a business trip," one wife explained. "What if the plane goes down? Will he accept the Lord as it's plummeting down to explode in fiery wreckage?"

Another woman, married to a man who works in the steel mills, feels acutely aware of his on-the-job hazards. "If he should die tomorrow, I don't think I could bear the idea of him being condemned for all eternity," she admits.

For many years, Bev worried each time her husband went out to race his sailboat on a not always pacific Pacific Ocean. But she knew, too, that he could be involved in a fatal accident on his way to or from work. What if it should happen before he accepted the Lord?

She finally realized the futility of continuing to live in a state of anxiety. Life, after all, is fraught with hazards, from the moment we get out of bed each morning till day's end. God doesn't want us to live in a prison cell of fear. He wants us to trust him. David must have understood this well when he wrote, "When I am afraid, I will trust in you" (Ps. 56:3).

Today, Bev believes with all her heart that God will save her husband before he dies—but of course that doesn't stop her from claiming the Lord's protection for him each morning.

If you are consistently troubled by this fear, keep in mind that, in a very loving way, God is aggressive in seeking a relationship with your husband. And if something should happen to him, somewhere away from you, the opportunity for him to receive the Lord would probably be there during his last moments. In circumstances where we can't know a person's heart, we simply believe that God is fully capable of a dramatic last-minute spiritual rescue.

*Does sadness fill my mind?* The great hymn, "When Morning Gilds the Skies," asks if sadness fills our minds, and for many of us, the answer is yes. Some of us do mourn for our husbands, knowing how their sins must grieve God, wanting so much for them to repent and be right with God.

"It was only when I began to realize, in a study of the beatitudes, that 'those who mourn' refers to those who mourn over sin, that I understood why I sometimes actually weep over my husband's behavior," Fran declared.

Nancy's sadness is rooted in the teaching of Jesus: "I tell you in that night there will be two in one bed; one will be taken and the other left" (Luke 17:34).

And she lamented, "Of course I want to go, but I have this vivid image of Jack left behind in bed, and I weep for him."

Other women feel a sadness over how much their husbands miss in not knowing the Lord. We see that if they would only turn to him, he could help them so much. That is why it is so hard to see our men struggling to make a living, to possess things, or developing ulcers in relating to the boss or on their climb up the corporate ladder. One man, engulfed in the mid-life crisis of realizing, "I'm over the peak; everything from now on is going to be downhill," expressed his frustration to his wife. "You would think that by now I would have some control over my life!" he moaned.

"Of course," his wife said later, "I know that the only truly satisfying answer for him would be not to have control, but to relinquish it to the Lord. I started to say something, but he didn't want to hear it, and I ached that he could not yet see the truth."

*God, give me patience—right now!* Bev feels both of us could probably write a book on patience! "I think it's my life lesson," she admits.

"Oh, groan!" responds Pat. "Learning more patience means having it tested—and that will require more waiting!"

We are doers, and when we see the answer to a problem we want to facilitate it, to make it all fall neatly into place.

If that is your nature, too, it is hard for you to wait . . . and wait some more. Won't your husband ever see the truth?

When Bev was in Brazil and became agitated over a "why hurry?" attitude, a resident of Sao Paulo passed along a wise saying of his country: "Wait sitting down."

David expressed it in another way when he wrote, "Be still before the Lord and wait patiently for him" (Ps. 37:7). David may have had an impatient nature, too. Oh, that we could internalize the pairing of these two words, "wait" and "rest," and learn to wait not in finger-drumming, foot-tapping agitation, but in a position of trust and rest!

Wait for who to act? God—not your husband! David emphasized this in his words, "But now, Lord, what do I look for? My hope is in you" (Ps. 39:7).

Our impatience doesn't help bring our husbands to the Lord one bit faster. But it will wear us out and put a tremendous strain on our marriages. We pray that God will help all of us to learn to trust him and to "wait sitting down."

*I feel so frustrated, angry, sorry for myself.* Sometimes it seems that the longer we wait, the less things change. Our patience wears ragged and feelings of frustration and anger mount till, as Stacey put it, "I just don't know how much longer I can stand it! I feel like I'm a time bomb, waiting to go off. My husband was ranting and raving last night about 'what hypocrites Christians are,' and my son is hassling me over 'all his friends' going to a punk rock concert. I've tried so hard to be a good Christian and nobody cares. Sometimes I feel so hurt, I don't think I can take anymore. Other times I get so angry that if I weren't a Christian, I'd leave."

When we experience this kind of pain, when we are ready to "stuff it" all, it is natural to look around for those at fault, those contributing to the problem. For us, there are several common targets.

*It's all my husband's fault.* Some may be tempted to say this. In our impatience, we may direct our anger at our husbands. "Oh! He is so stubborn! He just digs his heels in and will not be moved. If only he'd go to a Bible study, or read that book I got for him, or talk to my pastor, or come to church, or listen to what I'm telling him, or stop spending so much time watching TV. If only he'd just get with it! Yes, it's all his fault!"

Oh? Is it?

As we talked with women who have lived with unsaved husbands for years, we were surprised to discover that most of these men bear scars from hurtful past experiences with God, the church, or Christians.

Tom sang in the choir, but when the church split, he

stopped going. If Christians couldn't live together in unity, he wasn't interested.

Sam's mother, raising her kids alone, asked the church for help when she was in financial trouble. She was told she would have to sell her piano before the church would help. To young Sam, that seemed cruel.

Bill remembers how, as a child taking instruction to join the church, he told his teacher, "I really can't believe all of the Apostles' Creed." Her response: "That's OK. Say it anyway." Bill's conclusion: Christians are hypocrites and I don't want to be one.

When Joe was six his mother died. A relative, trying to bring comfort, told him God had called her home. Young Joe hated the God who took his mother when he needed her so much.

Men, once they have been hurt, usually are very slow to put themselves in a position of vulnerability again. As Dr. Douglas A. Wilson, of CORE Christian Counseling Center in Newport Beach, California, points out, men are basically more controlling than women; it is harder for them to let go, to seek help in any form.

Many of our husbands may need to be healed of such hurts before they can let go and come to the Lord. And that may be why God is so patient with them, allowing them to develop new concepts of him and his church through a loving relationship with us. Remember, we mentioned in the last chapter that values are changed over a period of time through intimate relationships.

Then there is another factor to consider. After explaining the work of the Holy Spirit, Paul wrote, "The man without the Spirit does not accept the things that come from the Spirit of God, for they are foolishness to him, and he cannot understand them, because they are spiritually discerned" (1 Cor. 2:14).

So, you see, it may not just be that he won't. Maybe he can't. At least, not yet—not until the Holy Spirit opens his understanding. So don't compound the problem by blaming him or allowing yourself to lapse into feelings of animosity toward him.

We don't only get angry at our husbands, Sometimes we think, *Why don't other Christians do more?* Surely the pastor could say more than hello to your husband when he does make it to church. And why did he have to preach on tithing the only time your husband came last year? Maybe if he would call on your husband—explain Jesus' death and resurrection to him. . . . After all, he is supposed to be the expert and he ought to have all the right words.

Then, if that elder who is in the same business as your husband would take the time to talk shop with him. Or why don't some of the men invite him to play golf or go to a baseball game? Wouldn't you think they could make more of an effort?

Well, yes, perhaps they could. Unfortunately, they are only fallible human beings—probably overworked men, at that.

And think back to how poorly your husband received some of the gestures others have made toward him. Of course, you want Christians to continue to try, but be honest; be fair. Don't make the church the scapegoat for your feelings of frustration.

Ultimately, most of us feel angry at God. Surely he made a mistake in bringing you together with this man. I mean, just look at how different you are. Was God, in fact, paying any attention at all, or was he simply looking the other way? Why doesn't he rescue you? Why doesn't he just zap this man of yours and turn him into a model Christian?

We forget that God gave us (and our husbands) a free will. We each must respond to him and choose to obey him. He won't grab us by the throat and force us. And we really wouldn't want him to, would we?

We need to be honest enough to look back and see if our sins are at least partly responsible for "this mess" we are in.

The Bible clearly tells us, "Do not be yoked together with unbelievers" (2 Cor. 6:14). The passage goes on to ask what fellowship righteousness can have with unrighteousness, or light with darkness?

That is a real guilt-provoker for those of us who were already believers when we married our unsaved husbands. Jan was active at church, but never had been taught it was unscriptural to marry an unbeliever. Besides, though Bill made it clear he would not attend church, Jan was sure when they were married she could change that. After all, he had never been to her church. Like many of us, Jan was wrong. Years later, Bill is still adamant about not going to church.

Some of us were slow to accept the Lord, and we married before we knew what the Bible says. Joanne came to the Lord when she was forty, after attending Bible study for a year with a friend. She and Sam had already been married for fifteen years.

It is possible, too, that we may have married during a time of rebellion or backsliding from our faith. Martha made a commitment to the Lord as a twelve-year-old, but drifted away during college. When she married during her senior year, it never occurred to her to care whether or not her husband was a believer.

Others of us were fully aware that it is wrong to marry an unbeliever, but were "so in love," or so convinced that we might be the one to save him, that we went ahead and married anyway. "I was absolutely certain that God put us together so that I could be the Lord's instrument to help lead him to the Lord," Janet confessed to us.

Still others of us, as singles, embraced the world's lifestyle and lived together with our men before our weddings. Perhaps we became pregnant and then decided we must marry.

A number of women whom we interviewed also felt that some other sin in their past is directly or indirectly responsible for the "state" they are in. Those who were promiscuous as teenagers or victims of rape or abuse sometimes feel they are being "punished," that they are disqualified or unworthy of the joy they would find in their husbands' salvation.

It is also possible that some of us were deceived, that our husbands pretended to be Christians just to marry us. Sonia told us her husband attended church and lied about being a believer before they were married. "He told me later that he wanted me so much, he would have done anything to get me." Now she wonders why she wasn't more discerning. Why didn't she ask God if this was the man he wanted her to marry?

For some of us, our problems aren't just rooted in the past. We turn our anger or frustration inward—at ourselves. As Joy put it, "The trouble is, I'm just not good enough. Not a good enough Christian. Not a good enough wife." We take on much of the responsibility for our husbands' being still unsaved.

This kind of talk is so destructive! It inevitably launches us into a downward spiral. We want so much to be the "perfect little witness!" So we lapse into despair each time we speak a harsh word or seek our own way. With a wife like this, we tell ourselves, it is no wonder our husbands don't come to the Lord! And the harder we try to be perfect, the more flawed our performance becomes.

But remember, our husband's salvation is not up to us. It does not depend upon how well you perform. Just as it is quite impossible to achieve it for him, when God decides it is your husband's time of salvation there will be little you can do to thwart it. As Kenton Beeshore, pastor of Mariners Church in Newport Beach, California, put it, "No one will be in the wrong place in eternity because you didn't do or say the right thing." God is perfectly able to reach our husbands in other ways. And in the meantime, we try to be good witnesses because we love the Lord, not because our husbands' salvation depends on it.

## IF WE CONFESS OUR SINS

During the research for this book, Pat realized she felt "more sinful" than certain other wives of unbelievers because as a

Christian she married an unbeliever, while other women became Christians a number of years after marriage. Then it dawned on Pat that although she had done wrong, she was no more sinful in marrying an unbeliever than some women who delay accepting the Lord, willfully resisting him.

We all need to realize that deciding who is more sinful or less sinful is a fruitless search. Sin is sin. God alone is the judge of what are bigger or lesser sins. What is important is that we recognize our sin and do something about it. We need God's forgiveness, and we must forgive those with whom we have been angry.

*The Holy Spirit can help.* Receiving and giving forgiveness sounds so simple, but it isn't always easy. Because guilt feelings are painful we have learned to hide them, even from ourselves. Yet they often lie deep within us, affecting our attitudes and feelings.

We need the Holy Spirit's help in sorting out our feelings and discovering the guilt and unforgiveness tucked deep inside us. Jesus promised us a Comforter who would show us the truth and that the truth would set us free. All we need to do is ask for his help.

When the Holy Spirit showed Martha how angry she was at her husband, she was appalled. She viewed herself as a kind, gentle person, the antithesis of an angry woman. Yet there were things her unsaved husband did that hurt her. In trying to be the good Christian, she let them pass, hiding her feelings, blaming all her problems on him. But inside her pain grew until she felt emotionally black and blue. The Holy Spirit showed her that her hurt was really anger that she was afraid to express, fearing it would not be Christian.

Whatever sins the Holy Spirit shows you, simply confess them to the Lord and he will cleanse you. Remember God's gracious promise in 1 John 1:9—that if we confess our sins, God is faithful to forgive us and to cleanse us of all unrighteousness. Note the word *all*. He didn't say part of it, but all of it. Think about it! That is such an overwhelming promise that it takes time for it to come alive in the many facets of our lives.

Then we need to forgive those we have been blaming: our husbands, other Christians, and God. The Lord knows how hard this is for us, and will work with us if we ask.

Finally we must make peace with ourselves. How? By accepting the forgiveness God provided for us. We must let it flow deep inside of us, changing our attitudes toward ourselves. That means no more trying to be good enough to earn forgiveness. It is a free gift from God. No more self-punishment, self-pity, or putting ourselves down in an attempt to pay for our sins. No more telling ourselves that we are not worthwhile. As the expression goes, "God don't make no junk!"

*Confess to another.* You will also find it helpful—and it is definitely scriptural—to talk with someone whom you trust. Or, as the Scripture suggests, "Confess your sins to each other and pray for each other so that you may be healed. The prayer of a righteous man is powerful and effective" ( James 5:16).

Neither of us could have dealt with our anger without the listening ears and prayers of a few friends. And we still need this help from time to time when the problems of being married to unbelievers threaten to overwhelm us again.

Finally, we need to bear in mind that when God forgives sin, he doesn't even remember our sin, for he promised us, "I, even I, am he who blots out your transgressions, for my own sake, and remembers your sins no more" (Isa. 43:25).

As forgiven Christians we rest in the assurance that there is no condemnation—that is, no sentence passed, no punishment—for those who are in Christ Jesus (Rom. 8:1).


## THE BIBLE PROMISES US

But we still long for our husband's salvation or maturity, and can't help wondering at times if it ever will happen. Fortunately, we have some wonderfully reassuring scriptural promises to hang our hopes upon.

*He is sanctified!* The Apostle Paul wrote, "And if a woman has a husband who is not a believer and he is willing to live with her, she must not divorce him. For the unbelieving husband has been sanctified through his wife" (1 Cor. 7:13-14).

Here is a truly mind-blowing promise—that our husbands have already been set apart unto God! This is one of those, "I don't understand it, but God said it, so it must be true" passages.

At the very least, it means that our husbands have been set apart for special treatment by God, that he will see they get whatever help they need to eventually trust their lives to him. Some even believe that this passage assures the husband's salvation, but that view seems to go beyond the teaching of other Scriptures concerning our free will, which God does not violate. We may not comprehend all this verse says, but we can claim the promise and rest in it.

*Remember the Philippian jailer.* When the Apostle Paul was jailed in Philippi, as he and Silas prayed and sang hymns to God, suddenly an earthquake shook the prison. All the doors flew open and everyone's chains came loose. But none of the prisoners left. The jailer was so amazed that he fell trembling before Paul and Silas and asked, "Men, what must I do to be saved?"

They replied, "Believe in the Lord Jesus and you will be saved—you and your household" (Acts 16:31). The verse suggests that when the jailer believed he apparently opened the way for the rest of his household to come to the same faith. If it was true of the jailer's household, why not ours?

*God's desire for us.* What do you feel is God's desire for your husband? Scripture offers us the assurance: "But do not forget this one thing, dear friends: With the Lord a day is like a thousand years, and a thousand years are like a day. The Lord is not slow in keeping his promise, as some understand slowness. He is patient with you, not wanting anyone to perish, but everyone to come to repentance" (2 Pet. 3:8-9).

Surely God is "not willing" for your husband to perish. In your eyes, his salvation seems to be taking forever. But the Lord cares about him, and is giving him more time to repent.

## LOVE HIM AS IF HE IS ALREADY SAVED

Jesus said to his disciples, "Therefore I tell you, whatever you ask for in prayer, believe that you have received it, and it will be yours" (Mark 11:24).

Gwen claimed this promise as she determined to love her husband and treat him as though her prayer for his salvation had already been answered. "I was amazed at the difference it made," she recalls. "I was no longer walking on tiptoe. It released me to share in an unpressured way. I even felt comfortable at one point in asking my husband to pray about a concern I had for our son. And one evening he asked me if I had prayed that day for our boy."

This is a perfect example both of God's power and of how people often tend to mirror the way they are treated. We have all seen the child who has been told he is a bad boy so many times that he begins to behave badly, to live up to his "job description." So, too, the person who is treated as capable and responsible is likely to assume responsibility in a job in the home or the marketplace and to carry it off well.

Try loving your husband as though his salvation is an accomplished fact. This is not a pretend game, a form of "imaging" or a "positive projection" exercise, but a challenge to treat your husband with the love and respect you would show if he was already a Christian. His response just might pleasantly surprise you, too. But even if it doesn't, you will be amazed how freeing it can be for you.

## TRUST JUST A LITTLE LONGER

Your husband's salvation—it may well be more precious to you than your own life. Some of you, in fact, would be more than willing to lay down your life for him. We pray that this chapter has relieved some of your fear and anxiety and that you can "wait" in a spirit of rest and trust just a little longer.

How will the Lord do it? Most likely in ways we have not yet dreamed of. Won't it be exciting to see?

## QUESTIONS FOR FURTHER STUDY AND GROUP DISCUSSION

1. Look up these Scriptures:

> *Jeremiah 17:9*
> *Mark 7:21-23*
> *John 16:13*

Then ask the Holy Spirit to show you your heart and help you identify your motives for wanting your husband saved. If any of your motives are not godly, confess them and receive God's forgiveness. Share with your group as much as you feel comfortable expressing.

2. What methods have you tried to "get" your husband saved? What was your husband's response to each? Do you need to ask his forgiveness for any of your efforts? Share some of them with your group; then discuss how you would feel if you were the unbeliever and your husband tried these methods on you.

3. Are there other people with whom you have been angry, in relation to your husband's salvation? Look up *Matthew 6:14-15* to understand how important it is to forgive. Then ask God to help you forgive them. If your group is trustworthy and forgiving, confess your angry feelings to them and ask them to pray for you according to *James 5:16*.

4. Do you ever feel angry at God over your husband's lack of spiritual commitment? Have you confessed that to the

Lord and asked his forgiveness? Do such feelings make you feel guilty, condemned? Do you think God understands your frustration? Do you dare be honest with God and other people about your negative feelings toward him?

5. Has the Holy Spirit shown you any sins that helped you "get in this mess"? Confess them to the Lord and receive his forgiveness as he promised in *1 John 1:9*. Then you may want to confess to another person, as suggested in the chapter.

6. Look up the following Scriptures.

> *Ezekiel 18:32*
> *John 3:17*
> *1 Corinthians 7:13-14*
> *1 Timothy 2:3-4*
> *2 Peter 3:8-9*

With these promises, are you able to believe that the Lord wants your husband saved? If not, why not?

7. Share what you have learned from this chapter that helps you trust the Lord with your husband's salvation or growth. And if you are still struggling to trust, share your feelings and ask the group to pray for you.

**Pray together for God's forgiveness for your sin, for help in forgiving your husband, other Christians, God, and yourself. Then ask the Holy Spirit to give each of you the gift of faith to believe that your husband will be saved or will mature in Christ.**

# FOUR
# THE VIEW FROM YOUR HUSBAND'S SIDE OF THE FENCE

We have talked a great deal about the way our husbands' lack of commitment affects us. But what about their reactions to us and to the dramatic changes many of us undergo when we come to the Lord or grow in him? Our men promised to marry us for better or worse, but they may not be at all sure now which of the two we have become! Of one thing many of them are certain. We definitely are no longer the women they married.

## LET'S HEAR WHAT THE HUSBANDS SAY

We spoke with a number of husbands about their reactions to their wives' conversions and found several common threads.

*"Uh-oh! What's she into now?"* It was revealing to hear how many husbands referred to the "various phases" of their wives' lives. As one expressed it, "First it's yoga, and then it's symphony volunteer, and then aerobic dancing. A lot of things come and go. So when this one [her Christian commitment] came along and she began hotfooting it to church, I thought this was another passing thing. After a while, I figured she would go on to something else. But—surprise! She didn't."

If we have a history of moving from one interest or enthusiasm to another, no wonder it takes several years for some of our husbands to believe we are serious about our Christianity.

*Bewilderment.* "I couldn't imagine what had happened to my wife," Chuck admitted. "Suddenly she had her nose in this book called 'the Bible' all the time—I mean, when I left for work in the morning and as soon as we finished dinner at night. I thought it would pass, but she was really consistent. Then I began to wonder. . . ." He chuckled good-naturedly, "What could be more important to her than me? And I was baffled by the peace she seemed to be experiencing."

*"She doesn't need me anymore."* Bob said he worried that he might lose his wife. "She became so much more confident. She had always been so quiet and noncommittal that I found myself surprised at all she could verbalize. She had a new strength that I couldn't understand. I was afraid she didn't need me anymore."

Another husband expressed alarm at "how independent" his wife was becoming. "She used to discuss every little thing with me, almost lean on me for decisions. Now she seems so much more assured, able to step out on her own."

*Fear.* Other husbands begin to panic when they realize this is not a fleeting fancy, when they see the depth of their wives' commitment. Some fear that their wives have turned into "Jesus freaks" or become "weird." Joe teases his wife, claiming she has become a "holy roller" or one of those who "swing from the chandeliers." But it isn't all kidding. With the mass suicides at Jonestown and all the strange mind control cults around, he worries a bit about his wife's Christian affiliation.

*Jealousy.* Sometimes a husband feels jealous of the time a wife spends away from him, especially at church, where he knows there are other men with whom she can relate in a common faith.

And some actually believe they are in competition with God. A few may be so threatened, they become angry and defensive. Or as one expressed it, "I was afraid I might lose her to God. In fact, when she came back from a weekend retreat with her feet hardly touching the ground, if I hadn't known better, I would have said she had been off having an affair. And I guess in a sense, she had. She was truly in love with Jesus. Not only was that something I couldn't understand, but it made me wonder, where does this leave me?"

*Anger.* Tom felt he had a good marriage and that he and his wife shared many common interests—till she met the Lord. "Now," he laments, "she is moving farther and farther from reality. She wanted me to go to a Bible study with her, so I dragged off with her a couple of times, but what I was hearing there was just silly. I never thought we would be divided like this. And frankly, I'm mad."

Milt was furious because he felt his wife had changed the game plan of their marriage, since her priorities were now different. "She isn't any fun anymore," he complained. "We used to go out dancing and drinking, spent a lot of time partying with the crowd at the club after tennis or golf. She just doesn't like to do the things we have always thought were a kick. She has even lost her sense of humor. Everything's become so serious. She doesn't laugh at my jokes the way she used to."

Nancy's husband became so upset he threatened to divorce her if she didn't quit "all this Christian stuff." She told us, "I stopped going to church for six months, was careful not to read my Bible in front of him and, of course, I didn't talk about my faith. But then he found I still had a Bible and he exploded. I was scared, but I had to tell him I couldn't give up my faith even for him. The next day he saw his lawyer and started the paperwork for the divorce. I knew I could never satisfy him, and I needed Christian fellowship, so I started attending Sunday worship again and asked my friends to pray."

Several years have passed and they are still together. Nancy's husband continues to threaten divorce at times, but he has yet to follow through.

One husband reacted so vehemently to his wife's Christianity that he left his family and later told his daughters they must make a decision between God and him. His wife now realizes that "I over-sought the Lord and needed to be much more understanding of where he was coming from. I got so involved with the kids, I robbed him of the children's attention." She adds, however, "There were many other problems in the marriage, so I suspect if it hadn't been my faith, something else would ultimately have separated us. Still, I would handle it much differently if I had it to do over again."

It seems that men who become this irate about their wives' faith often have problems in other areas of their lives. Fortunately, they represent only a small number of unbelieving husbands.

*"It's great for her, but. . . ."* Many men feel comfortable with "whatever's right for you, dear. If it makes you feel better, great." Some actually encourage their wives to go to Bible study. Kevin was completely supportive when Sally joined Bible Study Fellowship.

"She had been working for many years before our marriage, and I thought she needed something to fill her time," he explained.

Bill, a lukewarm Christian for years, remembers he wasn't interested in his wife's Christian activities, but they didn't bother him either.

Jack's attitude is, "It's fine for you, honey, but don't you dare try to convert me, no matter how subtly. I don't need any crutches."

*"Don't bug me with your nonsense."* Most husbands immediately sense any attempts at manipulation or evangelizing. And they are extremely resistant to efforts to change them—or even implications that they should change. As Paul said to his wife, "I'm an atheist, and that's that. You knew this when you married me. I made my decision back in college, and I have no desire to explore the stuff. So don't try to cram any of this foolishness down my throat."

Wayne, who later received the Lord, put it this way: "In

my pre-Christian days, everything Christian was an irritant to me. My wife didn't have to do anything pushy. Just seeing her read the Bible or coming home to hear a Christian radio station on the air was annoying. Most of the time I didn't react, but sometimes—I'm not sure why—it would really bug me and I would blow up. Looking back, I can see it wasn't because she was doing anything wrong. The problem was mine—the anger inside of me."

Why are we surprised at these reactions? Remember, these men do not yet have spiritual discernment (1 Cor. 2:14). They are still of the world, and you are no longer conformed to the world. That is a big, basic difference! For "the world cannot accept him [the Spirit of Truth], because it neither sees him nor knows him" ( John 14:17).

## HOW MUCH HAVE YOU CHANGED?

Remember how you thought and felt before you became a Christian? We usually see ourselves as changing for the better as we grow in our Christian life, but let us see how just a few of the typical changes may affect our husbands.

Do you usually go to church on Sunday? For many husbands that ruins a perfectly good weekend. They would rather get away from it all, fishing or skiing or exploring the countryside. Or they wish you were at home helping them with their latest project—or weeding the garden. Some may resent being awakened on Sunday morning when you roll out of bed to go to church. Didn't you once sleep in with your husband—and perhaps prepare a special, leisurely breakfast or brunch?

You probably no longer laugh at sexual innuendos, dirty jokes, or wisecracks at the expense of God or other people. Swearing or using God's name in vain now may make your flesh crawl. Even if you don't say a thing, your facial expressions and body language telegraph your disapproval to your husband and what used to be a fun part of your relationship may now be strained.

It is likely that you no longer enjoy or feel comfortable with worldly partying, heavy drinking, or drugs. Your idea of a rewarding night out now may be a seminar with a Christian leader, a program of gospel music, or potluck at church with your friends. But your husband finds your friends boring. Besides, there is no way he is going to put himself in a place where he can be ambushed by overeager Christians.

Your personality is probably changing, too. If you had a temper, you may flare less often. If you were shy, you may be gaining more confidence. Even "good" changes—those he likes—may be unnerving to your husband. He no longer knows what to expect from you and the uncertainty can make him uncomfortable. Try to understand how un-fathomable and even threatening these changes in you are to him.

## STRIKING A BALANCE

Is it possible, then, to find harmony together when you and your husband have such different focuses in life? Yes, most husbands say, it is possible if a wife gives a husband time to adjust without pounding him over the head with her Christianity.

Although we cannot turn away from our faith to please our husbands, let us consider what we can do to partially counteract the negative effects of our Christian commitment on our husbands.

*Minimize those things that offend him.* Be creative in your church attendance. The author of Hebrews encourages us, "Let us not give up meeting together, as some are in the habit of doing" (10:25). But Scripture does not prescribe all the specifics of that fellowship. Most churches emphasize the traditional Sunday school and worship service on Sun-day morning. Many encourage attendance at Sunday and Wednesday evening services as well. That is a lot of time away from our unbelieving or barely believing husbands.

Both of us find our husbands are not offended by Sunday morning church attendance. For years we skipped Sunday school to avoid being gone too long. And we rarely make the evening services. Instead we rely on weekday morning Bible studies and prayer groups to meet our need for more intimate fellowship without offending our husbands.

Some wives find Sunday evening services work better for them because they can spend the earlier part of the weekend with their families. And Carol discovered a church in town with a Monday evening service, which left her free to spend every weekend with her husband on their boat.

Others tell us that for a season of their lives they are not able to attend church at all. After Gwen's fourth child was born, she found it impossible to get all of the kids together and into their respective classes in time for her to get to church. "I'm too much of a wreck," she admitted. "My husband won't lift a finger, and I don't dare complain or ask him for help. He would just say, 'If it's so hard, just stay home.' So that is what I do, but how I miss the fellowship! I am hoping in another year the kids can do more to get themselves ready and I can get back to church."

Bible reading offends some husbands. If it bothers yours, avoid reading the Word in front of him. Instead, choose times when he is at work or busy elsewhere in the house.

Be careful about spending too much time with Christian friends, especially time you would otherwise have with your husband. Watch out for long telephone conversations when your husband is at home. At one time Pat had to ask her friends to limit their calls to daytime when her husband was at work.

*Your number one human being.* When we received Christ, we made him Lord of our lives, but we can and should make our husbands the "number one" human being in our lives. Our husbands need to feel they are important to us.

One of the best ways to communicate this is by making time just to listen to him. When he wants to talk, stop what you are doing, look him in the eye, and listen. If he shares a problem, you may want to toss out a couple of ideas, but resist your "mother's instinct" to take care of everything for him. By "helping out" you may make him feel you have no confidence in his ability. Most of us can solve our own problems if we can bounce our ideas off a good listener.

You can also make him feel special by cooking that dish he loves, kissing him good-bye in the morning, or even walking him out to the car. And don't forget to welcome him with an enthusiastic hug at night. Try writing love notes on his lunch napkin or to put on his pillow at night or in his suitcase when he travels. We will explore some other expressions of love in chapter 6. Meantime ask God to give you additional ideas for making your husband "number one."

*A man needs to be needed.* With God in our lives, we often experience increased confidence. The Lord promises to be the supplier of all our needs, our strength and protector, and we no longer are so dependent on other people. The independence feels good, but our husbands were attracted to us in part because they wanted to take care of us. It is important that we continue to give our husbands the gift of needing their protection and care.

Appreciate your husband's efforts at earning a living. When did you last thank him for that? Be grateful for all that he provides for you instead of dwelling on what you don't have.

Ask him to help with heavy jobs. Don't turn him down when he offers to carry in the groceries. Of course, you could do it, but enjoy his effort to care for you. Encourage him to open doors for you, to pull out your chair, or help you on with your coat. And when he is wary about your driving at night or traveling alone far from home, don't resent his concern. He is simply fulfilling God's call to be your protector.

*Be sensitive and flexible.* Neither of us find our husbands resentful of our faith or of the time we spend in church. But we try to avoid activities that will disrupt *their* lives. We dis-

cuss any request for extra church involv
before we make a commitment.

We find, too, that we sometimes n℮
them. For instance, when we are on weeke℮
husbands, we don't always insist upon see℮
church. We can, after all, pray and worship anywher℮.
these special occasions, we feel it is important not to detract
from our husbands' enjoyment or their time away from the
daily grind.

## IT'S NOT EASY TO WITNESS
## TO OUR HUSBANDS

"I wish she'd just. . . ." Several husbands expressed a fervent
desire for their wives to relax, to respect them and their
right to choose for themselves. "I don't want to hear about
her faith," Milt explained. "I can't say that I'll never need it.
But I don't need it right now."

"Give me time," seems to be the message here. Or as we
have emphasized before, be patient, trust, and wait "for
God's time."

In his book, *Liberation from Loneliness,* David Claerbaut
points out that, "Trying to change others, even for the better, is not love." Claerbaut, a psychologist, sociologist, and
professor, also says, "Nagging at them, humiliating them,
and putting them down only tires you out, stimulates anger
in them, and makes them less likely to change."[1]

*What, then, can a wife do?* We spoke with several husbands
who came to the Lord after their wives. And without exception they pointed to the silent testimony of their spouses'
lives. Not that their wives suddenly became perfect, but
they were changed.

These women illustrate the "1 Peter Principle" that even
husbands who do not believe the word "may be won over
without talk by the behavior of their wives, when they see
the purity and reverence of your lives" (1 Pet. 3:1-2).

We pointed out in our chapter on expectations that we

n't change other people by direct action, but it does seem that all of us tend to change in relationship to the changes that occur in those who are very close to us. So as we develop godly character, our husbands will be affected.

Graham Kerr, of "Galloping Gourmet" television fame, tells in his taped testimony of the incredible change in his wife, who, he declared, "swore and shouted and frothed at the mouth, had a demonic temper," to the point where she was in danger of "being locked up." He could not believe the change in her: her peace, her quiet, and the amount of time she spent reading the Bible. It was not long before Kerr began reading "the red stuff"—Christ's words—in the Bible, eventually joining his wife in the Lord.

Not all of us experience or need such dramatic turn-arounds in our lives, but even small, subtle changes can have great impact in the hands of the Holy Spirit.

*You're not your husband's only witness.* It is important for us to realize that our husbands' exposure to things spiritual is not limited to home. We can take courage in the little seeds we see sown by others—the unique witnesses that are so gentle, so natural that our husbands readily accept them.

Those we have seen and heard over the years show God's amazing ingenuity with the unsaved. Because we have a loving God who is diligently working for our husbands' salvation, we think our husbands will have many such experiences, most of which we may never hear about.

Often, it is simply a matter of a helping hand, without any attempt at all at evangelizing. When Ted's neighbor watched him struggle to wheelbarrow cement from the cement truck to his backyard patio, the neighbor brought over a couple of Christian teens who had stopped by his house and they each took a turn with the wheelbarrow. They didn't work more than twenty minutes but they saved Ted an hour of hard labor.

Because of several such incidents, when the neighbor invited Ted and his wife for dinner, Ted accepted, even though he consistently refused invitations from his wife's

Christian friends. Later when the neighbor moved away, Ted surprised his wife by suggesting that they invite the neighbor and his wife out for a good-bye dinner.

Steve was impressed when, following his wife's back surgery, her church friends supplied dinner every night until she was on her feet again. At first he was on his guard, thinking they would surely try to corner him. But they just popped in each evening with the food and a cheery greeting, then were on their way.

Sometimes the best witness is a job well done. Joe Stewart was so pleased with the workmanship and efficiency of the Christian contractor who built a vacation home for his family that he gave a party for the builder and his subcontractors when the job was finished. A year later, when he wanted to add some interior detailing, Joe and his wife found all of these men volunteering their time to build an addition to their church. "Hey, here are the Stewarts," the men exclaimed, stopping their work to gather around the couple and greet them warmly. "A great group," Joe declared as he and his wife drove away.

Occasionally, social situations that are sensitively and sensibly structured can work well. One woman gave a New Year's Eve party to which she invited not just one but several couples with unbelieving husbands and believing wives. She carefully focused the evening on having fun, not evangelizing.

More direct in their witness were the "love letters" one minister wrote to an unbelieving husband. But he began only after this skeptical spouse decided to attend church to find out what this Christianity was all about. During this time of searching, the pastor wrote him notes of encouragement, commending him for points of growth.

## ADD THEM ALL TOGETHER

Most of the Christian husbands we talked with agreed that "a lot of little things" combined to bring them to the Lord—in God's own timing.

We mentioned earlier in this chapter how Kevin urged his wife to go to Bible Study Fellowship. To further encourage her, he agreed to attend an evening Bible study with her. It was here that she made her commitment. Later, when members in the study assumed he was also a believer, he told them, "I'm not with you. I still have a lot of questions." He admits now that this was his cop-out, his block so "I could still do what I wanted to do."

He continued, however, in Bible study, till one late afternoon, after a day of hard yard work, he lay on the floor resting. "Suddenly, I felt the Lord's presence and I found that I really didn't have any questions. There seemed every reason to say, 'Lord, I want you in my life. I want you in charge.'"

Don's own children were quiet witnesses to him and "shamed him" into sharing some of his professional athletic abilities with their church youth group. "It was a very, very gradual turnaround for me, and it included an extended period of fence-sitting," he remembers.

Jackie's husband had been an angry man, extremely difficult to live with, and it was the change in Jackie, which came when she forgave him for all the past, that aroused his curiosity. He began going to church—but went by himself for an entire year. Then one day he made his commitment to Christ, and only then did he start going to church with his wife. A couple of weeks later, in Sunday school, he was asked to give his testimony. Jackie held her breath, but when he was finished there was scarcely a dry eye in the room.

On the other hand, Tad thought he was already a Christian. A couples' Bible study proved "interesting" to him. "I began to see there was much more that I hadn't put together. What I had were snapshots, as opposed to the whole movie. Our study leader suggested going to a Josh McDowell seminar on the Bible. And once I saw that the Bible is the authentic, inspired Word of God—that was it!"

More dramatic was the experience of Tom, an atheist who delighted in asking his wife impossible questions, such as, "Well, if God exists, why doesn't He make himself real to me?" He agreed to attend a Bill Bright seminar with his wife because it would be good for his business, sarcastically telling his neighbor as he left, "I'm going to get saved!"

His remark proved prophetic. For it was there that he read Isaiah 53, that unmistakable picture of Christ, written seven hundred years before his birth. "That did it! I didn't even have a choice," he recalls.

When we consider the diversity of ways in which these men reached the point of willingness to receive the Lord, we see how creative God is, how long and strong is his arm that saves. Be encouraged by his victories!

## WHY IS IT TAKING SO LONG FOR MY HUSBAND?

We asked Dr. Douglas A. Wilson, of CORE Christian Counseling Center in Newport Beach, California, about male-female differences in accepting the Lord. He noted that women are receivers, both physically and emotionally, and thus are more receptive by nature, less likely to resort to control.

Men, on the other hand, are basically more controlling; it is harder for them to let someone (or Someone) help them. Surrender, to them, sounds too scary. In Dr. Wilson's counseling, at least 66 percent of his clients are women.

And remember, many of our husbands have had experiences that left them with uncomfortable feelings about God or the church. It seems easier for women to understand and forgive these hurts than it is for men. With their more aggressive natures, they are less willing to make themselves vulnerable, to risk being hurt again.

## THANK GOD YOUR MARRIAGE IS INTACT

Perhaps your husband does grump at times about your Christianity, and of course, you would love to see him receive Christ. But have you considered how wonderful it is that, despite your tremendously different value systems, your husband still loves you, supports you, and wants to stay with you? Thank God for that, for any willingness he demonstrates to allow you to be your true self in Christ, and for all the things you *do* have in common.

## QUESTIONS FOR FURTHER STUDY AND GROUP DISCUSSION

1. Why do so many of our unsaved and barely believing husbands find our committed Christianity offensive?

> *John 14:17*
> *1 Corinthians 2:14*
> *2 Corinthians 2:14-16*

2. Were you surprised at how husbands view their wives' Christianity? Why? Did you see your husband or yourself in any of the illustrations in the chapter? Which ones?

3. Look up the following passages to discover some of what Scripture teaches us about church attendance and fellowship.

> *Genesis 2:1-3*
> *Exodus 20:8-11*
> *Mark 2:27*
> *Hebrews 10:23-25*
> *Acts 2:42-46*
> *Acts 20:7*

How do you handle your husband's irritation toward church and Christian activities? Are there activities you choose not to participate in because they offend your husband? (Notice that the Jews worshiped the seventh day of the week, but Christians met on the first day of the week. Perhaps it isn't the day that matters, but that we all have a special day of rest and worship to the Lord.)

4. Is it scriptural for us to make our husbands our number one human being?

> *Genesis 2:24*
> *Ephesians 5:22, 33b*

Discuss with your group how you feel about putting your husband above all other people. Share how you communicate to your husband his importance to you.

5. Many of the husbands with whom we spoke, who received Christ after their wives, mentioned the witness of their wives' godly lives. How has your life changed since you became a Christian? What Christian qualities are growing in you? Where do you still need to change to be obedient to Scripture? What helps us grow in obedience? Consider the following Scriptures before you answer.

> *Ephesians 4:20–5:4*
> *Romans 12:1–2*
> *Galatians 5:16-17*
> *Ephesians 2:4-10*

6. When we are disappointed with our marriages it is easy to focus on the negative, but the Psalmist reminds us to "give thanks to him" (Ps. 100:4). Make a list of the good things in your marriage and thank God for them. Then share them with your husband. Did thanking God change your attitude toward your marriage? How did your husband react when you shared with him? Share some of the good things in your marriage with your group.

**Pray together that each of you will be more able to see your Christianity from your husband's point of view. Ask God to help you let go of any desire to manipulate him into the kingdom of God.**

# FIVE
# CLAIMING OUR SPIRITUAL PRIVILEGES

Jill didn't know that when she was an infant her grandfather set up a trust fund to be paid to her when she turned eighteen. As that birthday neared, her father, trustee of the fund, worried. Would these thousands of dollars encourage Jill to be irresponsible? He considered not telling her about it, but ultimately decided he must, for the money was legally hers.

Jill was overwhelmed. "What a loving thing for Grandpa to do!" she exclaimed. "Why, I can go away to college after all. And someday it could help me start a business—or buy a home. Why, it gives me a whole new future!"

We as Christians have a priceless inheritance, not set up by our grandfathers, but by our loving heavenly Father. And it is infinitely more exciting in terms of our present and our future than Jill's. For it is an inheritance that Jesus has kept for us, and it brings with it spiritual privileges far richer than all the things Jill's money can buy. When we receive Christ it becomes ours, but like Jill, we must know about it to benefit from it.

## WHAT IS OUR INHERITANCE?

Our legacy is the privilege of a relationship with the Creator of all things, Almighty God himself. This relationship offers many benefits to every Christian. These can be especially meaningful to us as the wives of unbelieving and foot-dragging husbands.

*We have the privilege of being intimate with him.* Many of us were fortunate enough to grow up with devoted dads who, much of the time, loved us unconditionally. Now if we multiply that love, or the love we wish we had, to the highest power, we still can't begin to fathom how much God loves us, wants us to communicate with him, cares about our every care.

He is *Abba,* a term so personal that, according to *Vine's Expository Dictionary of New Testament Words,* slaves were forbidden to address the head of the family by this title. It is a word used by infants, similar to our word *daddy,* and indicates childlike trust, complete ease in the relationship.[1]

Knowing that God is our Abba Father—our loving heavenly Daddy—it seems so natural to talk with him. Francis Peeler, who, as a child, carried George Washington Carver's lunches to him, remembers that Carver would "stand at his window and talk to God just like I talk to you."

Peeler heard the pioneer scientist, looking out from his Tuskegee laboratory, holding a branch from a diseased tree, say, "Now God, you made this tree, you made this branch. Now—if you will—show me a way to cure it."[2]

Carver is not unique. Many other Christians have intimate relationships with the Lord. In *Practice of the Presence of God,* Brother Lawrence, a lay brother with the barefoot Carmelites in Paris of the seventeenth century, shared his desire to become aware of God every moment in everything he did. He called it "the habitual sense of God's presence," and told how at first it was very difficult to discipline his mind. He failed often, but eventually it became a habit.[3]

Both of us talk to God "just like I talk to you." We have not achieved Brother Lawrence's habitual sense of God's presence, but we talk with him often, from the moment we get up ("Thanks, Lord, for this day you have made"), through all the day's work ("Did you see how I blew that?

Help me, Father," or "Wow, Lord, did you see how beautifully that worked out? Thanks!"), to bedtime ("Couldn't have made it without you, Lord").

We encourage you to try it, too. Turn to him in all circumstances, with your joys, your disappointments—everything you feel. Picture him there with you in everything you do. Because you know, he really is.

And the most amazing part is that he has told us that is where he wants to be. Think of it: our Jehovah God, who is self-sufficient, self-existent, desires us to come directly to him in prayer!

*We are free to be honest with him.* It is our nature to hide our faults from others. It is not original with us. It began when Adam and Eve tried to hide their nakedness from God. But think how silly that was. God created them naked; he knew exactly how they looked. And he already knows the secrets of our hearts. In fact, he knows our "downsitting and our uprising," our every thought (Ps. 139:2).

Who else, then, understands us so thoroughly? Most of us frequently find our husbands either unwilling or unable to serve as our confidantes. And there are some things we are not comfortable sharing, even with close friends. So what a freedom—to be able to let down in complete honesty before the Lord, to pour out all our feelings to him and know there is no condemnation!

Tell him when you hurt ("Oh, Lord, I ache for my husband and his life-style"), when you're angry ("Can you believe what that man just said? Oh, Father, I am so furious; I'm ready to break every dish in this house!"), when you are discouraged ("Everything I touch today seems to turn to garbage. God, I'd like to dig myself a hole and crawl in!") We suggest that you keep short accounts. Whatever troubles you—when it troubles you—take it immediately to the Lord. Don't let it pile higher and deeper. This is especially important for you in defusing negative emotions that build from the frustration of being married to an unbelieving or barely believing husband. Honesty with the Lord is your birthright as his beloved child. Feel free to exercise it.

*We learn to listen.* We often pray and sing, asking God to help us to learn to listen for his voice. Yet often we are so busy talking to the Lord, we don't leave room for him to answer. We forget that the prerequisite for hearing is first to listen. This is a skill that may not come naturally, but one that most of us need to learn.

Dr. Frank Laubach, missionary to the Philippines and creator of the "Each one, teach one" literacy method, said in his diary *Open Windows, Swinging Doors,* "But this year I have started out trying to live all my waking moments in conscious listening to the inner voice, asking without ceasing, 'What, Father, do you desire said? What, Father, do you desire done this minute?'" His little book closes with the comment, "What a world gain if everybody could rest in the waiting arms of the Father and listen until he whispers."[4]

We find listening requires an open, receptive attitude toward God and time set aside when our minds are not concentrating on other things. For Bev, it means finding that quiet time and place where she is free from interruption. It might be in her "prayer chair" in her bedroom. Or it could be in her car, or even the shower, or while swimming laps in a pool. It is that space of time when distractions are removed, when we can calm our hearts and be quiet and open to the Lord.

Dr. Laubach told how, as he experimented in trying to be intimate with God, he verbalized aloud what God spoke to him, then wrote in his diary the things he felt God was saying to him. Pat has found it helpful from time to time to write letters to God and then to jot down the thoughts that sometimes come as God speaks to her inner being. These don't always come right away, but may pop into her consciousness later, while she is doing the dishes or going about the business of the day.

Most of us will never literally hear the voice of God. But he will teach us to recognize his voice in our thoughts, or as

Scripture says, in our hearts. The Scriptures promise: "He wakens me morning by morning, wakens my ear to listen like one being taught" (Isa. 50:4b).

How do we know whether or not it is the Lord communicating with us? How can we be sure we are not simply hearing our own thoughts, the answers we want to hear? Or could we even be hearing Satan? Discernment takes time and practice.

Be sure to check what you receive against the Bible. If it is from God, it will agree with Scripture. Also, Pat finds that God has a certain "tone of voice." If you are teachable, if you want to be obedient to him, he will be gentle and loving, never condemning or belittling. (Satan is the accuser—not God.) When you seek to hear God, he doesn't thunder at you. Notice that Elijah did not find the Lord in the wind or the earthquake or the fire. He heard "a gentle whisper" (1 Kings 19:11-15).

God sometimes asks hard things of us, and we may feel distressed at the challenge. But underneath—deep inside—we know the rightness of what we hear and it brings a peace.

Still, if in doubt, the Scriptures remind us: "Whether you turn to the right or to the left, your ears will hear a voice behind you, saying, 'This is the way; walk in it'" (Isa. 30:21). Give God time to make the answer clear.

It is our responsibility to do our best to listen, but we can ask him to help us hear and understand. We also might share with other Christian women what we think we are hearing, asking for their discernment.

Most of us do not listen well to people. We lose part of what is said or misunderstand the meaning even when we can see and hear the speaker clearly. No wonder we have such difficulty listening to God, whom we cannot see. Yet we are both convinced we can learn to hear and that the Holy Spirit is eager to help us.

In our particular situation, we especially need to hear from God, to discover his wisdom and his will for us in all facets of life—especially in relating to our husbands. It is an important key to being good witnesses to them.

## OUR INHERITANCE BRINGS RESPONSIBILITIES

With privilege comes accountability. To fully benefit from our relationship with God, there are a few requirements.

We must acknowledge that we are completely dependent on God. Sometimes we need to exhaust all our own resources, as many of us have done in trying to bring our husbands to the Lord, to come to that point of dependency. But this proves a wonderful place to be, for as the Lord told Paul, "My grace is sufficient for you, for my power is made perfect in weakness" (2 Cor. 12:9). Paul could rejoice that, through the power of Christ, in his weakness he became strong.

Next, we need to be obedient to God. Perhaps we can learn a lesson here from the Israelites, who, when they received the Law, promised that they would be obedient—and fell flat on their faces, again and again. We, in our own strength, no matter how hard we grit our teeth and try, will never be completely obedient. Only Jesus was truly obedient—obedient to death, even death on a cross (Phil. 2:8). But it is possible for us, through his Spirit working in us, to grow in obedience. And those times when we are truly able to yield to him, obedience seems to flow so naturally, and we feel such a sweet communion with the Lord.

In order to be dependent on God and obedient to him, we need to continue reading and studying the Word of God. "I don't know what I would do without this Bible study," sighed Julie. "The more I learn, the hungrier I am for more."

We hope the Bible is filling you with a similar enthusiasm. Of course, you can read the Bible on your own, and you should. But parts of the Bible are difficult to understand. So we find it helpful to get together with others to explore the Word, and further, we appreciate the discipline of a regular study. You will also find a variety of Bible study helps available at your local Christian bookstore.

We mentioned in earlier chapters the importance of fellowship with the body of Christ. For both of us, joining with other believers is absolutely essential. If your husband is not a believer, it is so easy to be sucked into the world's values, attitudes, and enthusiasms. But in Bible study and fellowship with other Christians we can focus instead on all the facets of our inheritance.

## I CAN BE AN INTERCESSOR
## FOR MY HUSBAND

Because we walk in the fullness of our inheritance with an intimate, honest relationship with God, we can become intercessors for our husbands.

Unfortunately, "When all else fails, pray," seems to be the motto of many today. If we become so absorbed in ourselves, our own efforts, and our concerns for our husband, we, too, may see God as our last resort, rather than our first.

Yet he loves us so much, it is his desire that we seek him first.

*It pleases God.* God delights in our intercessory prayer for others because it demonstrates our faith in him—that we believe he hears prayer, that he will hear our specific prayer, and that he can give what we cannot.

And he wants us to pray. God told the Israelites through Jeremiah that after their exile in Babylon, "Then you will call upon me and come and pray to me, and I will listen to you. You will seek me and find me when you seek me with all your heart" ( Jer. 29:12–13).

Jesus himself set a superb example of intercessory prayer for us. Isn't it mind-boggling to think that, though he is God, he prayed to his Father? John described him interceding for his disciples ( John 17), and Paul wrote that Jesus is now at the right hand of God making intercession for us (Rom. 8:34).

*Intercessory prayer is a privilege, not a duty.* "I feel just terrible," Jackie declared as she returned from a women's retreat. "We were so busy there, and our time was so structured, I didn't have time to really pray for the people in my family who don't know God. Usually I spend an hour each morning, as soon as everyone leaves the house."

Now it may be that God has called Jackie to a special ministry of intercessory prayer, and that she is disobedient when she deviates from her schedule. But we couldn't help but wonder if intercessory prayer had become an obligation—a heavy burden she tried to carry in her own strength.

For most of us, being an intercessor for our husbands—that is, one who pleads with God on his behalf—is a natural outflow of our love for our husbands and our love for the Father. We want with all our hearts to bring them together. It is as simple as that.


## WHAT DIFFERENCE DOES IT MAKE?

"How do I know my husband is one of God's chosen? What if my praying is all for nothing?" fretted Vera.

Jesus died for the whole world—which includes our husbands (John 3:16). And God does not wish "anyone to perish, but everyone to come to repentance" (2 Pet. 3:9). Moreover, the Sermon on the Mount shows that God, like a loving father, does not mock us. When we ask for bread he doesn't give us a stone, nor does he give us a snake when we ask for a fish. So we must not cheat ourselves out of praying for our husbands because we think that God might not care.

Oswald Chambers, in *Still Higher for His Highest,* explained intercessory prayer this way: "When we pray for another, the Spirit of God works in the unconscious domain of one's being about which we know nothing, and about which the one we pray for knows nothing; and after a while the conscious life of the one prayed for begins to show signs of softening and unrest, of enquiry and a desire to know something." He admitted that it may seem stupid to think that all this will happen, "but remember to whom we pray. We pray to a God who understands the unconscious depths of a man's personality, and he has told us to pray."[5]

## PRAY FROM YOUR HEART

Every pastor and teacher, it seems, has different guidelines on how to pray. Sometimes we become so bogged down with, "Am I doing it right?" that we think of prayer as a formula rather than a relationship with a Person who is alive.

For the two of us, what is in our hearts is the key. If you are overflowing with love for him today, then of course you will begin your prayers with adoration. If tomorrow you are moved by all that God is, you will want to praise him. But when your heart brims with need, bring it to the Lord, first thing.

That is what we see in David, a man whose heart was right toward God. Think how many of his Psalms follow a "pits to praise" format, beginning with "Oh, God, things just couldn't be worse; I'm hurting!" And after he's poured it all out, his spirit soars with thanks for God's help in the past, praise for his sovereign God, and hope for the future in him.

So pray for all the nitty-gritty daily things that concern you—your husband's growth, his faults, his success, health, and safety. Pray for any specific needs he has expressed to you.

Ask the Lord, too, to show you ways to love your husband better, to be sensitive to how you might help him. Entreat the Lord to heal any past hurts that may keep your husband from Christianity.

And seek the Holy Spirit to teach you how to pray more effectively for your husband.

Most of all, pray for God's perfect will to be accomplished, both in you and your husband.

## PRAY AS OFTEN AS YOU WISH

The Lord's parable about the man who came at midnight to borrow bread from his neighbor points up the importance of persistence in prayer—that we need to keep on asking, in spite of apparent refusal (Luke 11).

The teaching of the parable seems to indicate that we must pray every single day for our husbands, or even many times each day. Yet the Bible does caution us to avoid vain repetitions or reciting the same prayers over and over, "like pagans" (Matt. 6:7). It can get confusing, can't it? We can't reduce prayer to a formula.

That is why we emphasize praying as often as you wish. Your needs and circumstances, and your husband's, will vary, so of course the frequency of your prayers will vary, too. Certainly repeated prayers from the heart are not "vain" or in vain.

We believe you can also trust that the prayers you have prayed in the past still exist and will be answered. Our omniscient Lord knows and will not forget your heart's desire for your husband. Therefore there may be times when you pray very little for your husband. Rather, just rest, confident that God knows your heart and will respond to your prayers.

So pray for your husband's salvation when you are moved to do so, but be assured that if you don't pray every single day for him, God won't punish you by delaying his salvation another ten years! God is a loving Father, not a vindictive taskmaster.

## PRAYER CAN BE A WEAPON OF SPIRITUAL WARFARE

According to the Book of Job, Satan walked to and fro over the earth. He is still here, and it is possible that he is involved in the battle in your household. Paul pointed out that "Our struggle is not against flesh and blood, but against the rulers, against the authorities, against the powers of this dark world and against the spiritual forces of evil in the heavenly realms" (Eph. 6:12).

So that we can stand safe against all Satan's strategies and tricks, Paul urged believers to put on the full armor of God: truth, righteousness, the gospel, faith, salvation, and the "sword of the Spirit, which is the Word of God." Paul concluded, "Pray in the Spirit on all occasions with all kinds of prayers and requests" (Eph. 6:18).

Your prayers, then, can help frustrate Satan's efforts in your husband's life, pushing back the darkness, allowing the light of the Spirit to come in. You can even remind God that your husband has already been consecrated—made holy or set apart to him—because you belong to Christ.


## IS FASTING AN AID TO INTERCESSION?

Fasting, which means abstinence from food or drink (or both), can be a useful tool of intercession. For many it is an adventure in focusing prayer, in growing closer to God, and in seeing how he gives us strength when we need it. It is not for everyone, certainly not for those with physical problems that fasting could aggravate.

*Seek God's leading.* The key here is to ask the Lord. Seek his direction to determine whether or not fasting is his will for you. Certainly fasting is biblical. All Israelites fasted on special days, especially once a year on the Day of Atonement. And we know Moses, Daniel, Elijah, Esther, and David fasted in times of great need.

Jesus fasted forty days at the beginning of his ministry. The Pharisees and John the Baptist's disciples fasted regularly. But Jesus, when questioned as to why his disciples did not fast, replied, "How can the guests of the bridegroom mourn while he is with them? The time will come when the bridegroom will be taken from them; then they will fast" (Matt. 9:15).

There is no question then, that Christians—at least some of us—are to fast. But we each need to ask, "Is it for me, Lord?"

*Kinds of fasts.* Perhaps you think, as we once did, that fasting means no food or drink at all. This indeed is a common form of fasting. But there is also a partial fast, such as Daniel's when he apparently ate only vegetables, refusing the king's gourmet fare (Dan. 1:8-16).

*Why fast?* In her teaching on the Sermon on the Mount, Kay Arthur of Precept Ministries in Chattanooga, Tennessee, states that fasting is "earnestness of communion" calling us from "the mundane into intimate communication with him." It is never a means of manipulating God. Mrs. Arthur further states that fasting is usually born (of God) rather than instigated (by us) and that it stems from need, mourning, or sorrow.[6]

The Scriptures make clear that fasting does not please God unless it is accompanied by a life that is obedient to him (Isa. 58).

Fasting is useful in getting our flesh under control and it makes us more sensitive to God. We can fast to zero in on what he wants us to do, or to help us purify our motives. This makes fasting particularly useful in preparing us for spiritual warfare, when we think we may need to pray against the powers of darkness.

Fasting is appropriate, too, to beseech God for a specific outcome in a situation, or in asking for his help or protection. In other words, whenever you feel intensely about anything—the needs in your marriage, your husband's salvation—it is appropriate to bring it before the Lord, and fasting helps you focus on the need. You remember it every time you feel a pang of hunger!

*How to begin.* Although we have fasted a few times, neither of us feels called to extensive fasts. If you think the

Lord wants you to fast, we suggest that you start small. Begin with a partial fast or skip a meal or two. Later you might want to try a twenty-four hour fast from sundown to sundown.

Always consider prayer an integral part of your fast. Stay sensitive to the Lord and feel free to experiment. There are a number of good books in the Christian bookstore on fasting if you need help.

Finally, remember that Jesus told us in the Sermon on the Mount not to fast publicly, "as the hypocrites do, for they disfigure their faces to show men they are fasting. I tell you the truth, they have received their reward in full. But when you fast, put oil on your head and wash your face, so that it will not be obvious to men that you are fasting, but only to your Father, who is unseen; and your Father, who sees what is done in secret, will reward you" (Matt. 6:16–18).

## WE GROW THROUGH INTERCESSION

Do you wonder, sometimes, "What's the use?" You have been praying for many months—perhaps many years, and you really don't see great progress.

We believe God teaches us through this time of waiting and we challenge you to ask, "Lord, what would you have me learn?"

Someone said recently, "God is not in the business of making us comfortable but of building character." The word *comfort* as we use it rarely appears in the Bible. The framing, constructing, and finishing of our character is usually not a comfortable process, but pain with a purpose is quite different from "pointless pain." Contrast, if you will, the difference between severe menstrual cramps (pain seemingly without purpose) and the labor of childbirth (pain with a wonderful purpose—a baby!) God's purpose is glorious: to conform us to the image of his Son! (Rom. 8:29).

There are a number of ways we grow when we persist in prayer even though we see no progress. Most of these ideas came from teaching on intercessory prayer by Shannon Gustafson.[7]

As we pray for our husbands, we gain glimmers of God's perspective on our problems. We learn to believe in his wisdom, love, and power. Anna's story points this up. "Rick and I are so different," she told us. "I've struggled to learn how to relate to him and in the process I've learned a lot about men and marriage. Now I can see God's purpose in bringing us together. Other women seek my counsel. If we had been more alike, more comfortable, I wouldn't have had the struggle, but I wouldn't have learned what I needed to help others now."

As we pray for our husbands, God gives us the courage to persevere in spite of apparent refusal. As hard as this sometimes seems, it is part of the tribulation or rough way that James says gives our patience a chance to grow ( James 1:3).

As we pray for our husbands, we come face to face with our own helplessness. We see more and more clearly that we cannot answer our own prayers and therefore must surrender to God's will.

As we pray for our husbands, we must deal with our own selfish desires and ultimately align our will with God's. Donna realized that her husband came to the Lord only after she was able to see and declare to the Lord, "Father, my happiness does not depend on my husband's salvation. It depends on you."

As we pray for our husbands, we grow in trust that the Lord is doing something beautiful in our lives. Because of that we learn to praise God for difficulties and delays. Jackie waited more than five years for her husband to accept the Lord. She knew she was growing during that time, but had no idea how important that would be. Her husband, the son of a minister, knew his Bible and had participated in music ministry for years but had been turned off by the church.

Shortly after his total commitment to the Lord, he was asked to direct the choir and they found themselves part of the church leadership. "I wouldn't have been ready for that even a month earlier," Jackie admitted. "I needed all the time of preparation God gave me."

As we pray for our husbands, God increases our desire for his glory to be revealed. We learn he can bless more people and bring more glory to himself when we release to him the timing and circumstances of our husbands' conversion or growth.

Ultimately, Shannon Gustafson believes, we learn to be willing to say, "If you will do a deeper work in me by holding up [my husband's] salvation, it's OK."

Waiting, then, can change us—for the better!

*Asking others to pray.* Fellowship with other believers can and should include prayer support. We do not recommend asking for prayer in a group of two thousand and telling what a poor, depraved sinner your husband is. And it might also be best not to use your husband's name or yours when putting anything personal on your church's prayer chain.

Be sensitive about "uncovering" your husband with your prayer requests. When he does come to church, you don't want him or others to be uncomfortable because of what you have said in asking for prayer.

But we both do share in prayer intimately with a few people we trust, because we believe there is power "where two or three come together" in his name (Matt. 18:20).

*Pray with thanksgiving.* Paul exhorted believers, "Do not be anxious about anything, but in everything, by prayer and petition, with thanksgiving, present your requests to God. And the peace of God, which transcends all understanding, will guard your hearts and your minds in Christ Jesus" (Phil. 4:6-7).

We need to learn to pray for our husbands with thanksgiving. Too often, we let our anxiety steal our peace. We can offer thanks for our unsaved husbands, secure in the knowledge that all things work together for good to those who love him, to those who are the called according to his purpose (Rom. 8:28). That's us!

## TO GOD BE THE GLORY

When our prayers are answered, who gets the glory? Us? Our wonderful prayers? Of course not. It is God who answers—and God who will be glorified.

We must pray, "Not to us, O LORD, not to us but to your name be the glory, because of your love and faithfulness" (Ps.115:1).

Indeed, God promises, "Call upon me in the day of trouble; I will deliver you, and you will honor me" (Ps. 50:15).

Think what this means! The simplest, feeblest, most immature Christian can pray and pray effectively. It isn't a matter of great prayer, but of a great God. His is the power and the glory.

## OUR TRUST IS IN GOD

"Some of us put more faith in our prayers
than in the God
to whom we speak in our prayers."[8]

The foundation of our prayer life and of all our spiritual privileges must be trust in God and his sovereignty. Without it, we have built a house on sifting sand.

You know by now that you can't twist the arm or otherwise manipulate a sovereign God.

"I am God, and there is no other; I am God, and there is none like me. I make known the end from the beginning, from ancient times, what is still to come. I say: My purpose will stand, and I will do all that I please. From the east I summon a bird of prey; from a far-off land, a man to fulfill my purpose. What I have said, that will I bring about; what I have planned, that will I do" (Isa. 46:9-11).

What our prayers do accomplish, however, is to make God *our* God. Through them we honor him, exalt him, knowing that "Great is the Lord, and most worthy of praise" (Psa. 48:1).

We may not feel comfortable in our present situation, but we know that in his sovereignty, God is still in control.

In the beauty of the mountains of Mammoth Lakes, California, we held a small summer retreat for the wives of unbelieving and barely believing husbands as we began writing this book. Here is a Scripture we all claimed:

> *Commit your way to the Lord;*
> *trust in him and he will do this:*
> *He will make your righteousness shine like the dawn,*
> *the justice of your cause like the noonday sun.*
> *Be still before the Lord and wait patiently for him;*
> *Do not fret when men succeed in their ways,*
> *when they carry out their wicked schemes.*
> *Refrain from anger and turn from wrath; do not fret.*
> *Psalm 37:5-8*

## QUESTIONS FOR FURTHER STUDY AND GROUP DISCUSSION

1. Some of us feel disqualified from or unworthy of an intimate relationship with God. This feeling may stem from "terrible" things we have done or perhaps that have been done to us. If you struggle with such feelings, ask the Holy Spirit to help you understand their source. Remember, Jesus came and died that all our sins might be forgiven. Here are some verses that show God wants to forgive and restore.

> *Romans 5:8-11*
> *Ephesians 2:1-9*
> *1 John 1:9*

If you still feel as if God couldn't forgive you, read the stories of the woman at the well ( John 4:6–30), the woman with the alabaster box (Luke 7:36–50), the woman caught in adultery (John 8:3–11), and Paul, the killer of Christians (Acts 7:55–8:4; 9:1–16). Could any sin be worse than these? Yet Jesus forgave them. Share your feelings with another Christian who will pray for you. Then decide to accept God's forgiveness and trust that eventually your feelings will agree with your decision.

2. In the chapter we talked about Abba Father, our loving heavenly Daddy. Describe a loving daddy. Be as detailed as possible. Can you picture God as this kind of daddy? If you found it difficult to picture God fulfilling any of the characteristics of a loving daddy, ask the Holy Spirit to show you why and to free you to receive your "Daddy's" love.

3. How can we know if we are hearing God? List the guidelines mentioned in the chapter and repeated in the verses below.

> *Proverbs 15:22*
> *Romans 8:15-17, 26-27*
> *Hebrews 4:12-13*
> *James 1:5*

Share with your group examples of hearing God, and talk over any questions you have.

4. Is it important to God that we become intercessors? What does he do when we fail? What are some of the specific prayers you have prayed for your husband?

> *Isaiah 59:1-2, 16*
> *Romans 8:27, 34*
> *1 Timothy 2:1*

5. Here are some passages where people fasted. Why did they fast in each case? How long? What did they give up?

> *2 Samuel 12:13-23*

*Judges 20:18-28*
*Esther 3:13–4:3, 15-17*
*Jonah 3:4-10*
*Acts 13:1-3*

Share your experiences with fasting.

6. Read *Isaiah 58:3-12*. Why doesn't God honor some fasts?

7. Look up the following passages:

*Proverbs 3:5*
*Matthew 6:25-34*

Now find "trust" in the dictionary. How much do you trust the Lord in your situation? Does trust mean you don't do anything, but sit back and wait for God to change your circumstances? Does it mean you never worry? What are we supposed to do when we feel anxious? Is trust a feeling or a decision we make?

**Pray that God will teach each of you how to become more intimate with him and how to hear him more clearly. You may want to join hands in a circle and pray for each other to become skilled intercessors for your husbands. Then ask God for the courage to completely trust him in your situation.**

# SIX
# WHAT KIND OF
# WIFE AM I
# SUPPOSED TO BE?

You have read a lot thus far about how important it is for us to wait and trust and pray. We really can't just leap in as a one-woman spiritual SWAT team to save our husbands. But still, perhaps there is a part of us that longs for action. What can we do to help our husbands? What sort of wife are we called to be?

Scripture gives us two important roles to consider: home-maker and helper. Of course today we women are not limited to these roles. But they are important to our husbands. Bear in mind that none of us will achieve perfection or turn overnight into Mrs. Proverbs 31. We won't do all of what we are suggesting, all of the time. The Bible tells us, "Where there is no vision, the people perish" (Prov. 29:18, KJV). But we find very little that is worthwhile ever happens without establishing goals. We all need a mark (or marks) to reach to-ward. Let us examine some goals that should be ours.

Pat once asked her husband if anything particularly bothered him about her Christian commitment. He replied that he didn't care about the time she spent at church. No, he didn't feel he was in competition with God. What did bother him, he finally admitted, were the dishes that some-times stack up on the end of the sink or the pile of clothes left on the bedroom floor instead of in the laundry basket.

Bev received a similar communiqué. Busy planning and supervising a women's retreat for her church, she let the housework slide. Several days elapsed before she headed for her desk. There, inscribed in the dust on the file cabinet she found the words, TOO BUSY. Had her husband written it— or one of her sons? She wasn't sure and she didn't ask!

In both cases, the message seems clear: while we worry about being wonderful spiritual models, our husbands' outlook on what a wife should be is far more down to earth.

So let us begin with some practical reminders. Then we will move along to loftier levels.

## HOMEMAKING: YOUR MEMO OF LOVE

A century ago, John Ruskin wrote, "The true nature of home—it is the place of peace; the shelter, not only from all injury, but from all terror, doubt and division."

Isn't that the sort of place to which anyone would delight to return?

What—and who—will make your home a place of peace? Chances are, it will be up to you to create that environment, whether you work outside the home or not. Men, as we saw earlier, are not natural nest builders. Dr. Joyce Brothers points out that even if their wives work full time, most men do very little around the house.[1] We wonder if they even see what needs to be done.

This attitude in men that simply leaves homemaking to women is common in other cultures, too. We think God gives a man the burden to provide and protect his family. But he gives a woman nest-building instincts, a special sensitivity to her surroundings so she can make her home a pleasant place for her family to live. This means you can take both the responsibility and the credit for setting the tone of the home and making it a refuge for your husband and all the family.

All of us are busy and have countless demands on our days, whether we work outside the home or not. You will need to decide what matters most to your husband and to you, and be willing to let less important details go or do them less frequently.

*Neatness counts.* When it comes to housekeeping, most men to whom we spoke were like Pat's husband—more concerned with order than with operating-room cleanliness. Certainly they wanted a house that wasn't filthy. But deliver them from the Mrs. Clean who continually cautions the family to be careful or keeps everything under plastic wrap, making the home sterile and uncomfortable! What they craved after the confusion of the workday was some order at home.

Many of us learned this early and found it a huge challenge when we were at home with preschool children. Pat stopped the children's play to get everyone to help pick up a half hour before her husband was due. That was the time, too, to wash faces, comb hair (including hers) and perhaps put on a clean blouse. Bev remembers, "It was astonishing how much we could pick up between the time we heard his car in the driveway and the moment he stepped through the front door!"

Some men have particular peeves. "Most people think my house is extremely neat," Joan told us. "But my husband is bugged by the stack of reading material I tend to accumulate by my bed."

"Mine really comes unhinged when I let my incoming mail get out of hand," Terry noted. "I could get on his case about his workbench in the garage, but really, that doesn't affect me, and George sees the piles of paper in the kitchen at every meal."

Though it may seem strange to you, your husband may interpret your neglect in picking up as a lack of love for him.

Good homemaking takes time. Be careful of excessive church commitment or overcommitment in anything that will steal too many hours from your housekeeping. We are out of balance if we become so weary in well-doing that our husbands and our homes become secondary in our lives.

*Make dinner a time of restoration.* Did you know the term *restaurant* is rooted in the word, *restaurare,* meaning to restore? In your family "restaurant," why not make it your number-one priority to revive flagging bodies and spirits? Serve wholesome food, keeping in mind always your husband's likes and dislikes. How you serve a meal is every bit as important as what you serve. Strive for a pleasant setting. Try to make the plates colorful. (A wedge of orange and a bit of dark green romaine can relieve even a plate of cauliflower, sliced turkey, and mashed potatoes!)

Then, do everything you can to create a climate of calm. It is not always easy to shift from the overdrive of bringing a meal together down to a low gear of relaxed dining. And it is particularly maddening when you race at breakneck speed to get dinner ready, only to wait—and wait—while everyone takes his own sweet time getting to the table.

A few deep breaths may help before you sit down. Or better yet, stop for a moment and ask the Lord to help you ease up and to take away any resentment you are feeling. Tension and anger at mealtime tend to spread from one person to another, but so too does a sense of calm.

Watch for opportunities to inject a light touch now and then. Sometimes we become so deadly serious about our Christian walk and our husband's salvation, that we lose our sense of humor, forget to laugh at ourselves. When did you last bring a chuckle or even a smile to mealtime with your family?

Make an effort, too, to keep dissension away from your table. This isn't our natural inclination, because dinner may be the only period during the day that the whole family is together. But this is not the time to bring up the mean thing Tommy did to Susie or to bombard your husband with how terrible your day was or to insist that he fix the screen door right after dinner.

Proverbs states it well: "Better is a meal of vegetables where there is love than a fattened calf with hatred" (15:17).

*But homemaking is so boring!* A Canadian study indicated

that young women facing the decision of family versus career perceive the life of the homemaker as unglamorous and boring but see no alternative if they desire a family.

Of course, many women today find they must work. But for those of you who are able to choose, we want you to know that homemaking can be a rewarding profession. After our children were born, we both faced the dilemma of whether or not to have careers outside the home. The decisions weren't easy, but we both decided to keep our families our first priorities.

However, Bev didn't want her mind to vegetate, so after resigning her job as advertising copywriter when her first son was born, she immediately began writing free-lance magazine and newspaper articles and had a regular restaurant column for years.

Pat, who was a physical education teacher, felt the need to supplement the family income. She continued to substitute teach for many years and taught swimming to neighborhood children during the summer. Now she works a few hours a week for her brother-in-law, paying the bills for his building supply business. She also taught women's Bible studies for twenty years.

Today, with grown children, and a grandchild for Pat, we have no regrets. We have sometimes worked long hours to keep up with part-time jobs, deadlines, and home, but we have loved the luxury of discretionary time—time we decide how to spend—how our husbands long for that!—and the opportunity to explore different avenues of expertise.

Here are just a few of the "domestic" areas we have studied or participated in—no, not all at once—through the years: growing herbs, vegetables, roses, fruit trees; flower arranging; creating hanging baskets; cooking (from barbeque to microwave to Chinese); bread-making; cake decorating; needlepoint and knitting; sewing children's clothes and our own; furniture refinishing and upholstering; slipcovering; making draperies; interior painting; wallpapering; pottery-making; journaling; family photography; and youth group leading. And, of course, we have spent countless rewarding hours sharing with our children. It is hard for us to imagine any "outside career" that could be more fulfilling.

If you find yourself fearing or resenting the "bo-o-o-r-ingness of homemakin'," whether you do it full or part time, don't let it get out of hand. Relieve the monotony by learning a new skill or stretching your mind with work or study that you can do at home. You will feel much better about yourself, and you will be a far more effective and more interesting wife and mother.

## WE ARE CREATED TO BE OUR HUSBAND'S HELPER

After the Lord placed Adam in the Garden of Eden, he said, "It is not good for the man to be alone. I will make a helper suitable for him" (Gen. 2:18).

*Helper* is a difficult word for some women. It makes them feel put down, perhaps because it brings to mind the outmoded term, *hired help*. But remember, that passage also indicates that men need our help. Statistics bear this out. Dr. W. Peter Blitchington in his book, *Sex Roles and the Christian Family*, tells us that "single men die six times as often as married men from accidental falls and car accidents. They simply have less reason to protect their lives from accident and mishaps."[2] They also have more emotional problems and insomnia.

Many of us who raised sons have seen firsthand how truly helpful a relationship with a special girl can be for them. The transformation from selfish, reckless playboys into serious, responsible students and workers is beautiful to behold.

We see our helper role as a practical arrangement that God made, understanding that women are a bit more adaptable than men and more sensitive to the needs of others than most men. Think about it. Aren't you usually more willing to shift plans, and don't you cope better with sudden changes than your husband? And don't you usually zero in on others' feelings—especially nervousness, depression, anxiety—much more quickly than your husband?

These are the qualities God gave you, which equip you so well to be a helper. But what exactly does that mean? The whole concept takes on a new dimension when you look at the original Hebrew word. It is *ezer,* which stems from the verb *azar,* a primitive root that means "to surround, i.e., protect or aid; help, succour."[3]

What a beautiful idea—surrounding your mate with your love—helping to insulate him, to protect him when he comes home from the pressures of the day.

## SUBMIT? DO I REALLY HAVE TO?

If *helper* is a red-flag word to some women, *submit* can be a three-alarm word—especially at a time when many women are so intent upon claiming their "rights." Yet submission is an essential part of our role as helper. We know that it is taught in Ephesians 5:22 and Colossians 3:18. The Apostle Peter wrote clearly to the issue: "Wives, in the same way [that is, the same way as Jesus submitted to his enemies and entrusted himself to God] be submissive to your husbands so that, if any of them do not believe the word, they may be won over without words by the behavior of their wives, when they see the purity and reverence of your lives" (1 Pet. 3:1).

"But to submit is just so degrading!" Karen protested. "I'd feel so reduced as a person. Why can't we be equals, instead of the wife under the husband?"

You are equal before God! When you submit to your husband, you are to do it "as to the Lord." Are you a second-class citizen when you submit to the Lord? Of course not. A nuclear scientist doesn't become a second-class citizen because he submits to the President of the United States, does he? Well, neither is there anything "lesser" about you when you defer to your husband. Both men and women, as God's children, are heirs of God and joint heirs with Christ (Rom.

8:17). Jesus in his ministry never demeaned women or treated them as inferior.

Submitting is not a doormat position. Submitting to your husband does not mean lying down for him to walk all over you, or groveling and allowing him to wipe his feet on you. Nobody loves a doormat! And it doesn't mean worshiping your husband. He is not the Lord of your life; Christ is.

Men, striving for self-esteem and headship, sometimes seem to demand doormat obedience. And their wives, in an attempt to please their demanding husbands, may give up all their own wishes and even their own personalities. They lose their uniqueness and, in a sense, become a nothing. But men rarely like a woman when she gives in completely. How can they respect a namby-pamby "Yes, dear—whatever you say, dear" wife?

In Ephesians 5, Paul commanded believers to submit to one another. Then he spoke in detail of submission in three everyday relationships. He directed children to obey their parents, and fathers not to provoke their children to wrath. He commanded slaves to obey their masters, and masters to treat their slaves well. He told wives to submit to (Note he doesn't use the word *obey*) their husbands as to the Lord. And he admonished husbands to love and care for their wives as their own bodies.

We see, then, that Paul didn't want a wife to relate to her husband as a child to a father or a slave to a master. In verse 33, he spells out further the kind of submission a wife is to willingly give to her husband. It is called respect!

So don't put your brain on hold. Don't, in your effort to be a godly wife to an unbelieving or barely believing husband, smother your own needs, desires, and sense of values.

*Finding a balance.* The key to avoiding the doormat syndrome is to keep a balance between our helper and our submission roles. If we go overboard as a helper, we may become his "mother," nagging and bossing—for his own good, of course. On the other hand, if we become submissive to the point of losing our identity, we lose ourselves, the unique qualities that originally drew our husbands to us. To fulfill God's call to be our husbands' helpers, we must express our opinions and the intensity of our feelings to our husbands. Most husbands, as good executives, learn to appreciate their wives' input, as long as they are assured their spouses are not trying to become the boss.

In Peter's writings, Sarah stands as our example of submission (1 Pet. 3). Twice, in Genesis 12 and 20, Sarah told a half-truth at Abraham's request to protect his life—and landed in a king's harem. She trusted God and Scripture tells us God protected her. Now, that is submissive!

Yet Sarah was also very bold and open about her desires. She told Abraham what she wanted done about Ishmael's mistreatment of her son Isaac (Gen. 21:10). She was submissive because she didn't kick Ishmael and his mother out herself, but she wasn't a doormat, allowing the abuse to continue. Notice that God told Abraham that Sarah was right.

So why does God say the husband is to be the head? God has written a wonderful marriage manual in his Word. You may be surprised to know that it also dovetails beautifully with all that psychologists and anthropologists are learning today about male-female differences.

We discussed earlier the fact that a man tends to be more aggressive than his wife. That extra competitiveness helps him to be a successful provider and protector for his family. But he also needs to be head of the house to fulfill these responsibilities. For example, he must choose a place for his family to live where he will be able to provide food, clothing, and a roof over their heads. It also must be a place where he can protect his family (in our society he often looks for a location with good law enforcement). Although of course his wife will have input regarding the home, it is important that she be sensitive to his desire to have his family in a place where he can take care of them.

But remember, his headship doesn't give him the right to coerce or force his wife into submission. The biblical example for headship is Christ, who always served and worked for the good of those he led. Note that Jesus invites us to follow him, but never forces us.

*Competing for leadership.* As we seek a balance between being submissive and not being a doormat, we may find ourselves competing with our husbands for the right to make decisions.

So who should make the decisions in marriage? Will it be the one who is strongest? Or lasts the longest? Or yells the loudest? Or even the one who says the nastiest things about the other?

"We spent ten years of our marriage competing for leadership," Dora recalls. "And it didn't work at all. We fought over almost everything. And it was so difficult to feel loving toward one another when we were mad at each other half the time."

Dora's comments point up the important fact that it is almost impossible for us to love someone we are battling. And men, who are aggressive and competitive by nature, find it even more difficult than we do. No one wins when we compete for power in our marriages.

Most couples gradually divide the responsibilities in the marriage. For example, often the wife is responsible for the meals and the husband takes care of the cars. Each then makes the decisions related to his or her realm of responsibility. However, what about areas that concern us both and where we don't agree?

We find it best to give in or compromise when possible and only make a stand on those issues that are most important to us.

*But my husband isn't a believer.* Perhaps you feel you cannot submit to or respect your husband because he is an unbeliever. Or possibly you think this biblical passage is addressed only to Christian couples.

But it is for you, too, because it is a game plan that establishes order in the home. It works, whether your husband knows the Lord or not, because it is based upon the basic, essential natures of men and women.

## RESPECT: THE KIND OF SUBMISSION AND LOVE MEN NEED

The complaint of comedian Rodney Dangerfield, "I don't get no respect," echoes the sentiments of many husbands.

Yet Paul made it clear that respect for our husbands is vital. Paul told all Christians to submit to one another. But note the difference in the kind of submission he asked of the husband and the wife. He told the husband, "Each one of you also must love his wife as he loves himself." But he instructed the wife to "respect her husband" (Eph. 5:28, 33).

God made women with a need to be loved with caring and tenderness, or as it is expressed in Ephesians 5, the way a man loves his own body. He made men with a deep need for respect. To men, to be respected is to be loved.

Showing respect may not be natural for us. The problem that arises here is that all of us tend to give what we want. We are a little like the five-year-old who presents his mother with a frog for Mother's day. Because as women we have such a deep need for hugs, tenderness, all the little demonstrations of love, this is what we are likely to give to our men.

Meanwhile, what men really crave is not so much the expression of our affection, but evidence that we honor them, value them, approve of them. This is essential to their self-esteem.

And when men are told to love their wives, they tend to love as they would like to be loved. But that leaves their wives still hungering for the caring tenderness they need.

Now, this makes about as much sense as a woman giving her husband the string of pearls she would adore for Christmas and him giving her the fishing pole he wants.

*Respect means esteeming our husband.* Now, that may seem an old-fashioned word, but we use it in the sense of prizing him, setting a high value on him. It doesn't depend on what he *does*. It means recognizing each man's worth as a person created by God. You need to let him know what a treasure he is to you, how important he is in your life.

It might be a simple, "I'm so lucky to have you." Or you may even be able to share, "God was so good when he gave you to me!" Or, "I'm truly blessed to be married to you! Thanks for putting up with me."

Even in a difficult marriage, you can find some reasons to value your husband. Ask the Holy Spirit to show you how much he values your husband.

*Respect means showing our approval.* Respect is saying, "You look absolutely fantastic in that brown suit." It is re-marking, "I'm sure glad you haven't let yourself get paunchy and flabby." It's admiring his strength, ("I could never have moved that couch without you,") and his mind ("I can't believe you've figured this out already"). It is prais-ing him for all he does to provide, protect, and love you.

Of course you don't approve of everything about your husband, but dwell on the positive. You may find it helpful to remember back to what attracted you to him in your dat-ing days. Tell him about it. And express your appreciation for all he does for you now. Thank him for making it possi-ble for you to take a satisfying vacation. Tell him he is great in bed. Show him how grateful you are for his handiness around the house.

*Respect means honoring your husband.* And often that can mean watching your tongue. Be careful what you say to others about your husband. When you ask for prayer for him, is he honored or exposed? Be sure that, like the ideal woman of Proverbs 31, your words are wise and kindness is the rule for everything you say (v. 26).

Before you open your mouth, ask yourself how your hus-band would react if he should overhear you. Gene Molway, a pastor in southern California, had just such an opportu-nity. He walked into the house to hear several neighbor-hood women in the kitchen complaining about their husbands. Then his wife began, "Well, my husband. . . ." Gene waited, fascinated, wondering what she would say, ". . . is just wonderful!" she declared.

That is respect.

If you are having difficulty in the area of respect, listen to a woman who has been married for more than twenty years to an unbeliever. "I really respect Billy Graham and if he ever came to my house, he would get red-carpet treatment. When I asked God what to do to make my husband happy, he told me to treat him as though he were Billy Graham!"

Treat your husband as if he were the person you most respect, not because he always deserves it, but because the Lord commands it.

## A GENTLE AND QUIET SPIRIT IS PRECIOUS TO GOD

To really understand the challenge of submission, we must consider 1 Peter 3 because it gives us the reason for submitting to our husbands: "so that, if any of them do not believe the word, they may be won over without words by the behavior of their wives, when they see the purity and reverence of your lives" (vv. 1–2). Peter goes on to cite the importance of the beauty of "your inner self, the unfading beauty of a gentle and quiet spirit, which is of great worth in God's sight" (v. 4).

*Strong's Exhaustive Concordance* says the Greek word for "gentle" ("meek" in the KJV) means humble.[4] It is the opposite of arrogance, argumentiveness, or defensiveness. Outwardly, gentleness may be confused with weakness, but true gentleness requires great inner strength.

Strong pointed out that the Greek word for "quiet" means peace, and by implication: still, undisturbed, and undisturbing.[5] We are not talking here about silence but a settled quiet of the heart.

The only way we can achieve either of these qualities is to fully trust the Lord. In our own strength they are impossible. No wonder God considers them precious. We may not think we are physically pretty, but these qualities bring a kind of "deep beauty" that continues to make us attractive to our husbands long after physical beauty fades.

*Why was Peter concerned about inner beauty?* In *Tried by Fire,* a commentary on 1 Peter, F. B. Meyer pointed out that in the early church the Holy Spirit showed no partiality but endowed women equally with the men. Many women responded to Jesus and became Christians after their marriage. There was considerable hesitancy in the early church as to their duty under these circumstances. Ought they to leave their husbands? Change their behavior toward them? Assume any superiority over them?

Meyer wrote, "'No,' said the Apostles, 'stay where you are. . . . Be chaste, gentle, loving, submissive, winsome so that hearts may be softened, which have never heard a word of Gospel preaching, and may be won by the beauty of your holy and unselfish lives.'"[6]

## A WORD ABOUT OUTWARD BEAUTY

We think inward beauty is far more important and enduring than outward beauty. Furthermore, it is available to all of us. But we can't ignore the fact that men are visually oriented, which is one reason many are girl watchers. While you work on building a beautiful character, also do what you can to keep yourself outwardly attractive. Your husband may see some "very well put together" women where he works. So allow time to at least brush your hair and dab on some lipstick and blusher before breakfast. Before dinner, freshen your makeup and slip into something attractive. Even your "relaxing" clothes can be flattering in color and line.

## THE GENTLE SPIRIT IN COMMUNICATION

As we listen to Christian talk radio programs, again and again we hear wives complaining about the lack of communication in their marriages. Communication isn't easy, especially over the hurtful places in our relationships. But it is so unhealthy and unproductive to hold on to this pain, to live with anger and resentment. Of course, we must forgive our husbands, but we also need ways of expressing successfully to them what we feel. So how do we get through to our husbands and how do we help them to open up to us? One key is to learn skills in keeping with a quiet and gentle spirit. Here are a few suggestions.

*Nagging is not "gentle."* The writer of Proverbs pointed out that "a quarrelsome wife is like a constant dripping" (19:13b). Don't be a wife whose words drip, drip, drip like a leaking faucet. What do you do when faced with the annoyance of that maddening, repetitive, discordant "plink, plink, plink-plink?" You have two solutions: to tune out or to get out, right? Try to remember that as you watch yourself for repetition. And listen to your tone of voice. Is it louder than necessary, strident? Quiet is the by-word. Easy does it. And consider this: even if a man recognizes the need to change, nagging makes him feel rebellious.

*Be direct and clear.* Men are generally not adept at picking up hints, innuendoes. Don't expect your husband to be a mind reader. State your message in a few simple sentences. Use examples. For instance, "I'm feeling really pressured right now. I need to spend extra time with my mother while she is ill. Could you help with grocery shopping once a week?" Even if he is unwilling to do as you ask, he may come back with a compromise suggestion.

*Sandwich suggestions between praise.*[7] Men are often quick to pick up on a tone of complaint. Try to keep the overall tone of your message positive. There is always something for which you can commend your husband.

*Use "I" messages, not "you" messages.* Make the framework for your communication how you feel—not what he doesn't do or does wrong. Translate "You never take the trash out," to "I feel angry when I'm left alone to carry out those heavy trash cans."

Say things in a way that leaves the final choice to him. It isn't loving to trap him into doing things your way. Try, "Have you considered . . . ?" Or, "I wondered if . . . ?"

*Learn to express your anger in a feminine manner.* Paul wrote:

"In your anger do not sin" (Eph. 4:26). The initial anger is not the sin, but what we do with it may be.

In any marriage there will be times when we are hurt. And even though we forgive, it doesn't mean we must pretend we felt nothing. Whether it is your husband's fault or not, how will he understand if you don't let him know what you really feel?

If you find it difficult to confront, you might work toward expressing your anger while emphasizing the masculine/feminine differences between the two of you. Often if you appear smaller and weaker, your frankness becomes less threatening to your husband, helping him let down his emotional walls and "hear" your true feelings.

One approach is to exaggerate his larger size. For instance, if he is sitting, kneel beside him so you are looking up at him, rather than standing so you look down on him.

Some women use exaggerated threats. Pat's favorite is the wife who declared, "I'm so angry, I'm going to get a telephone pole and hit you over the head." Of course her husband laughed, but you can bet he understood she was frustrated. The impossibility of such a threat emphasizes a woman's helplessness, expresses her anger, and, surprisingly, is usually very appealing to her husband. A husband instinctively wants to take care of his wife.

Another way to express anger is to call him names. This sounds juvenile and un-Christian, doesn't it? But hear us out. The key is that the names must make him feel more masculine. Many men are rather pleased to be called a bully, stubborn, or perhaps even a hairy ape, because these "insults" imply strength and aggressiveness. But they also communicate your anger.

*Learn defusing techniques.* Do you sometimes flare without thinking, going for the jugular with the meanest cut you can devise? Have you ever tried expressing that anger to the Lord first? Jerry recalls, "I would really let my husband have it—tear him into shreds. And then I would feel terrible. I learned finally to take all the mean things I wanted to say to

112

Steve and cry them out to the Lord. It was amazing how little I had left to tell Steve afterwards."

To handle spur-of-the-moment anger, try repeating your husband's statement back to him. "Somehow, this buys me time to gain some cool before I respond," one wife pointed out. "Sometimes it even calms him, to hear his own words repeated."

*Choose your times to talk.* When you have been stewing over something all day, the natural tendency is to spill it all on your husband the moment you are back together again in the evening. Do try to resist that temptation. Wait till your husband has a chance to, as one husband puts it, "get my toes unbraided." Some men listen much better after they have eaten. And don't try to discuss important issues when your husband is in a rush or worried about something else.

If you need to work through a truly serious matter, you might make a date with him: "There's something I really need to talk to you about and I wonder if we could go out, just the two of us, for a bite to eat (or dessert, a Coke, coffee) on Wednesday night. Would that work for you?"

Talking about difficult subjects in a public place may keep a discussion from escalating into an argument, but be careful. Your husband may resent it if he feels trapped or manipulated.

Open communication may open spiritual doors. Whether our husbands come to the Lord or not, we will have better marriages if we improve our communication skills. And how in the world can we expect to express Christ to them if we can't communicate on other basic issues of our lives together?

You must keep sharing your feelings with him—about everything, including church and your walk with the Lord. But share from the standpoint of, "This is what is going on in my life," with no attempt at evangelizing or coercing.

We often feel this isn't enough, that it won't make a difference in their lives. But Jesus demonstrated this sort of restraint with his disciples when he told them, "I have much more to say to you, more than you can now bear" ( John 16:12).

## THE PAY-OFF OF THE GENTLE SPIRIT

Cary told us there had been several troublesome areas in his marriage until his wife, Linda, became a Christian. "Little by little, those problems seemed to go away as she began to rely on God. I watched her grow into such a sweet person, so willing to serve! She was just so—good—about things. Never demanding, never expecting anything of me, she just gently pulled me along, even though my feet were dragging."

Eventually, Cary began going to a Bible study with Linda. The turning point for him came when he committed to join with the group in praying for a family whose child had died in surgery. The next morning, while jogging, he asked the Lord to come into his life.

## ABOUT YOUR ATTITUDE

Are you feeling overwhelmed with all we have suggested—that you would have to be Wonder Woman to accomplish all this? As we told you in the opening of this chapter, none of us will be able to do it all. What matters far more than what you actually do or say is the feeling you transmit—whether it's one of "hafta do all this" or "want to."

Paul urges us to have a mind or attitude like Christ, "Who, being in very nature God, did not consider equality with God something to be grasped, but made himself nothing, taking the very nature of a servant, being made in human likeness. And being found in appearance as a man, he humbled himself and became obedient to death—even death on a cross!" (Phil. 2:6-8).

Who are we to say we can't or we don't want to serve another person—our husbands—when Christ willingly came as a servant to all of us?

A minister gave an example of a servant's heart as he told

of a converted wife who despaired of her husband ever knowing the Lord. She said she was afraid her husband would never get to heaven, so she made up her mind to make him as happy as she could in this world.

Although we do not feel this despair for our husbands and we pray that you don't either, this wife's attitude of making her husband happy now could bring a tremendous difference in our relationships with our husbands.

In *Building a Great Marriage,* author Anne Ortlund suggests as the building block of a great marriage the question, "What can I do to make you happy?" Urges the author, "Ask it over and over. Ask it the rest of your life."[8]

However, some men have such melancholic temperaments that very little makes them happy. But there is a step in serving beyond trying to make your husband happy. Think what a blessing we would be if we could pattern the rest of our lives after the woman of Proverbs 31:12, who brings her husband "good, not harm, all the days of her life."

## QUESTIONS FOR FURTHER STUDY AND GROUP DISCUSSION

1. What evidence do we have in Scripture that women are called to be homemakers or keepers of the home? Look up the following verses and add any others you can think of:

> *Proverbs 31:10-31*
> *Titus 2:3-5*

2. Can a working woman also be a homemaker? What difficulties does she have to overcome? And today, what kinds of problems does a woman encounter when she chooses to stay home with her family?

3. What creative approaches and activities have you tried to bring you satisfaction and keep homemaking from becoming boring? Bring samples of your creativity to your group,

if you can. Do you have techniques that cut down on the work of homemaking?

4. How do you feel about being your husband's helper? And about submitting to him? Are there limits on how far we go with these roles? Discuss the differences between being a doormat and a submissive wife in the scriptural sense. Which ideas in the chapter were helpful to you? Do you disagree with any points?

> *Genesis 2:18*
> *Ephesians 5:23-24*
> *1 Peter 3:1-2*

5. Sarah is our example of a submissive wife.

> *Genesis 12, 16–17, 20–21:21*

How did she fit in with her husband's plans? When did she express her own feelings? How have you fit in with your husband's plans? Are there times when you express your negative feelings to your husband as Sarah did? Share examples with your group.

6. What are the differences in the way men and women need to be loved? How do you show your husband that you love him? Which of those ways communicates your respect to your husband? Is respect a feeling or a decision of the will? Is your husband aware of your respect? Is it right for a Christian wife not to respect her husband? What if he doesn't deserve respect? Read *Ephesians 5:25-33*.

7. Read *Philippians 4:8*. Then make a list of all the excellent things about your husband. Share your list with him. Perhaps you would like to write them in a love letter or maybe put one each day in his lunch box. Watch his reaction. Some men have never felt their wives' respect and may be very moved by it. Has dwelling on your husband's good points given you warmer feelings for him?

8. Describe in your own words the "gentle and quiet spirit," mentioned in *1 Peter 3:4* that is so precious to God. Are there times when you live your description? Where do you fall down? Ask the Holy Spirit to help you grow, and you may want to ask your group to pray for the areas where you repeatedly fail.

9. Have you tried any of the communication skills suggested? Which have been helpful to you? Which are you hesitant to try? Why? How about using a new one this week?

**Pray for the Holy Spirit's help in your homemaker and helper roles. Particularly ask him to help you respect your husband and to become a better communicator in your marriage.**

# SEVEN
# BUT WHAT HE
# WANTS IS WRONG

Consider the following scenario. As Ellie and Kurt head from their car toward the supermarket, Ellie drops her shopping list. Stooping to pick it up, she sees from the corner of her eye the brown envelope nestled in the bushes of a planted divider.

"Wonder what this is," she murmurs. Kurt leans over to watch as she picks up the thick packet and releases the metal clasp. They both gasp as she pulls out a rubber-banded stack of money.

Grabbing it from her, Kurt swears softly as he thumbs through the bills—fives, tens, twenties, and look here—some fifties and hundreds. "There's gotta be several thousand here!" he exults. He glances nervously around the parking lot. "Stuff it in your purse."

"We'll have to turn it in, Kurt," Ellie says quietly.

"Turn it in!" he shouts. "Are you out of your mind? Think what it would buy!"

She knows he is thinking *boat, trip, fishing equipment*. For a moment she lets her mind drift, too. Braces for Sally. Maybe a new refrigerator. No, she tells herself. Meals for the hungry. Help for our church's building fund.

She shakes the thoughts out of her head. What is the matter with her? They can't keep that money.

Kurt has her by the arm now. His grip makes her wince. "Finders keepers," he mutters. "Not a word about this."

Have you ever had an experience like this, where your values and morals clashed with your husband's? Probably it didn't involve thousands of dollars, but still, these situations can create painful, even frightening, crises in the marriage of the believing wife and the unbelieving husband.

Some of you are fortunate to have married a man with a background compatible with your Christian values, so you share the same ethics. But there are so many like Ellie.

Tammy, for example, loved her husband's "grab-for-the-gusto" attitude when she first met him. "He comes from this wild and crazy Bohemian sort of family where anything goes, as long as it feels good and you can get away with it," she explained. "At first, I thought it was all great fun. But now that I know the Lord, I'm having problems. It's obvious to me that a lot of what he does—and wants to do—is just plain wrong."

Where do the difficulties tend to arise?

## THE COMMON PROBLEM AREAS

*Money Matters.* "What about taxes?" someone asked. "Do I sign if he's cheated?" The dilemma most frequently mentioned by wives is the preparation of the income tax. "We have a small business and my husband saves the stubs from all our restaurant checks and claims them as a business expense, even if not a word about the company has been exchanged," Jerry complained.

"We depreciated a certain percentage of my car as a business expense for three years, and that was legitimate," Flo recalled. "But then my husband insisted upon depreciating his new car for my business, even though I continued to drive only my own car."

Of course, none of these may be go-to-jail transgressions, but the Bible tells us there is no such thing as "little sins." What are we to do? Then there are the cases where the cheating is more blatant—for instance, when a husband regularly takes payment for his services in cash and "forgets" to report it as income.

Who decides how money is spent? It has been said that the number one cause of arguments in any marriage is money—what to spend, how to spend it, what to save, and even *if* to save.

One young woman recalled, "I was brought up in a home where nothing was ever bought on credit—not even a car. Oh, yes, there was a mortgage on the house, but that was it. Enter my husband, the big spender—of money we don't have." She ticked off on her hand the payments they must make each month: the car, television, video recorder, microwave, and a boat for water skiing. "Now my washer is kaput, and we'll have to buy that on time, too."

Her friend nodded. "And oh, the bills that have to be paid every month when you buy on time! Ours stack up and up. My husband doesn't seem to be concerned, but I'm worried sick."

"My husband didn't save money for our kids' college education and now Jeff is a senior in high school," his mother lamented. "My husband insists he should go to a classy college on the east coast that will land him a good job. Do you know what that costs every year? I say Jeff can get a good start on his education at a community college here, earn some money, and then transfer to a state university. We don't see it the same at all."

Tithing and other giving may also become a sticky area. If you have a career outside the home, you may be able to tithe from your income. But if your career is making a home for your husband and raising the children, it may be difficult to ask a staunchly unbelieving husband for money for the church or for favorite Christian causes.

*Your social life.* Someone asked concerning office parties: "Am I conforming to the world if I go? I can't begin to tell you how I hate Dan's office parties—especially the Christmas blowout," Phyllis declared. "There's always some little secretary passed out or being sick in the ladies' room. I hate all the boozing, the noise, the smoking, the off-color jokes, the guy who always makes a pass at me. My husband looks forward to it—has a perfectly wonderful time, with a hangover the next day to prove it."

Phyllis says she vacillates each year between the desire to support her husband and her distaste for the debauchery, the feeling that she is becoming part of the world.

*Heavy drinking and drugs.* Some men love to center their social life on cocktail parties, meeting friends at the local pub, tapping a keg, or sharing a six-pack in the backyard. If you joined in the fun in your pre-Christian days and now abstain, you may come across as a goody-goody, a damper on the fun. Some men will allow you to quietly sip your Coke or Perrier water. Others—and their friends—may make life miserable for you.

Even if your church doesn't call for complete abstinence, chances are you are offended by the dependency of your husband and his friends on alcohol or drugs for "a good time."

*Sexually offensive social activities.* One wife noted that "the big rage these days seems to be bringing in a stripper—male for the women and female for the men—whenever someone's celebrating a birthday or a promotion." Also cited are the "characters" for hire who enliven a party by coming on to the evening's honoree with a barrage of sexual patter.

And how about the concept of "open marriage" or even wife-swapping that is a part of social life in some circles? That can be a confrontation time for a Christian wife.

*Extravagance.* Partying and keeping up with the social whirl is costly. "My husband took me to an opulent restaurant with crystal chandeliers and footstools for the ladies," Dee recalls. "The whole menu was a la carte and he just loved being addressed by his name, waited on hand and foot, finding our car sitting at the curb when we left. The check for two of us was more than a hundred dollars. I literally felt sick, thinking about all the hungry people that money would feed."

*Recreation and vacations.* Some husbands' idea of recreation is an evening of lurid jokes at the Laugh Club or a girlie show in a seamy neighborhood. And perhaps a trip to Las Vegas and hours around the gaming tables and the slot machines is his concept of a vacation.

"I hate it and I don't know whether to stay home and leave him to the predatory females out there or to go and act like it's all OK," Tina complained.

## THEN IT ALL HITS HOME

It is difficult enough when our values differ on conduct and morals outside the home. But when it is right there in our living room or our bedroom we wonder if anything is sacred anymore.

*Pornography.* One of the biggest "thorns" for wives in today's society seems to be the television channels that invade their homes via cable with R- and X-rated programs. Lorrie described, "For five years we had one of those illegal 'black boxes' that brought pornography into our home. I tried to watch with my husband a couple of times but I didn't know which was more disgusting—the sickeningly graphic programs that had no dramatic value—or the way my husband sat and practically drooled. Worst of all, they would hype him up till he was just an animal, hauling me off to bed." Lorrie was delighted when the channel's signal was changed and they could no longer pick it up.

Other women grate at the pornographic magazines and posters their husbands bring home (and sometimes display), sexually graphic gifts designed to turn the wives on, and sensual lingerie they are expected to wear.

*Swearing.* Difficult, too, for many women is their husbands' profanity. Some, like Peggy, complain, "He cannot complete a sentence without a swearword. I mean, he can't even say it's a nice day without swearing. I'm ashamed to bring any of my friends to the house, and I hate the way our kids pick up on it."

Another woman declared, "Mine only swears when he's angry, but then the air literally turns blue. And then I become so angry at the way he profanes the Name of the One I worship . . . I simply have to get out of there."

*Drinking and smoking.* Next on the women's list of at-home hates were heavy drinking and smoking. "I just cringe," Joanie admitted, "when the kids come in and see their father passed out on the couch." And Millie lamented, "Even my clothes stink of his cigarettes and, worst of all, his cigars. And the way *he* smells . . . Yuck!"

*In the bedroom.* We are convinced that behind the bedroom doors of many homes lie some rather miserable women. It is not that they are prudes or frigid or have Victorian standards. The problem is that their husbands want—and sometimes demand— responses that are truly repugnant to the women.

As one wife agonized, "I'm told to submit to my husband. But what he wants to do is not enjoyable for me at all and sometimes it's even painful. Am I still obligated to do it?"

Another problem area arises when husbands pass along their sexual standards to the children. Bill, who firmly believes that all men should have sex before marriage, told his boys that they could do whatever they wished sexually—as long as they were honest with their partners. That wasn't their mother's stance at all, but how could she, a female—and especially a mother who didn't sound like any fun at all—possibly counteract the boys' father's advice?

## HE LACKS CHRISTIAN CHARACTER

*He lies.* "Lord, Lord, how this world is given to lying," Shakespeare noted in King Henry IV. Indeed it is, and while some of us catch our husbands in exaggeration (the proverbial fish story or war story that becomes embellished with each telling), others find that lying has become a contagion in which one lie begets another.

"He lies to cover up his mistakes, to save face, to make himself look better—and sometimes, I think, just to see how much he can get away with!" Marty exclaimed. "The hardest part is that once you realize this, you lose trust. You don't know when to believe him."

*Other men steal.* "I am almost certain that the expensive watch my husband 'found' was stolen from a locker at the gym. I'm sick about it, and this isn't the first time this sort of thing has happened," Terry revealed.

*Some men play around with other women.* Susan saw her husband's car parked outside a motel at noon one workday. "This is something I absolutely can't handle," she wept. "I'm devastated."

So many differences in values and standards! Where—and how—can a woman draw the line?

## LET'S LOOK AT SCRIPTURAL PRINCIPLES

We wish we had simple answers, a quick formula to handle these areas of difference between you and your husband. But truthfully we can't tell you exactly what to do. Your situation is unique, you are unique, and your husband is unique. What we can do is point out some of the scriptural principles that will help you decide what is right for you.

*We are to be obedient to the Lord.* The Bible uses the words *obey* and *obedient* eighty-five times in the Old Testament, forty-one times in the New Testament.

It is clear that our first obedience is to the Lord. This is exactly what Peter and the other apostles told the Sanhedrin. "We must obey God rather than men" (Acts 5:29). Paul cited as our model Jesus, who was obedient even unto death, even death on the cross (Phil. 2:8).

In the Old Testament God showed us through Saul an example of a man whose obedience was not complete. The Lord had clearly told him to strike Amalek and utterly destroy all that he had, including the animals. But Saul and his men spared the best of the sheep, oxen, and lambs. His excuse? "I just took them to sacrifice to the Lord."

Samuel's response to Saul: "Does the Lord delight in burnt offerings and sacrifices as much as obeying the voice of the Lord? To obey is better than sacrifice, and to heed is better than the fat of rams" (1 Sam. 15:22).

*God appointed our husbands head of the household.* Look again at what we learned earlier about headship. All Christians are called to submit to one another, and submitting to our husbands is part of being obedient to the Lord, but it does not supersede our allegiance to the Lord. Remember, Peter promised us it would help win our unbelieving husbands to the Lord.

Helping our husbands is another part of God's plan, and we must find the true meaning of helping and submitting. We are not his helper if we submit to the point of saying nothing in areas of conflict. Our husbands need our carefully weighed opinion, the wisdom of our knowledge and experience and to be aware of the intensity of our feelings. Thus it may be important to tell them when we think they are doing something wrong or when they need to do something right, as Sarah did when she went to Abraham about Ishmael's mistreatment of Isaac.

Because your husband has been given by God the responsibility of heading the household, often but not always this means he will make the final decision in areas where you do not agree. Without this principle your home becomes a battlefield, with both partners struggling for their own way. Love cannot survive such strife.

God knew when he created this order for your home that your husband wasn't perfect and was bound to make mistakes. So don't expect him to be always right. There will be times when you, as his helper, will graciously cover those errors, if you can. But be cautious about always trying to rescue him from the consequences of his behavior. God may use the circumstances to speak to him and help him grow through his mistakes.

## WHEN BIBLICAL STANDARDS
## SEEM TO CONFLICT

When our husbands want us to do something that violates one of God's commands, what should we do? For example, what if your husband wants you to lie for him? Your alternatives appear to be either to refuse to submit or to lie. Scripturally you are wrong either way. When two of God's commands seem to oppose one another in our lives, we must seek God for a better way. James reminded us, "If any of you lacks wisdom, he should ask God, who gives generously to all without finding fault, and it will be given to him" (1:5).

Many times with God's help we can come up with a third alternative, rather than simply deciding that we must either defy or comply with our husband, thus doing one or the other of two wrongs.

Jesus was a master of creativity when faced with what seemed a no-win situation. Remember when the Pharisees tried to trap him by asking if it was right to pay taxes to Caesar? If he had said yes, the Jews would have been angry with him, and if he had said no, the Romans would have accused him of rebellion. Recognizing their intent, he asked whose name and picture were stamped on Roman coins. "Caesar's," they replied. "Well, then," Jesus said, "give it to Caesar if it is his and give God everything that belongs to God." His reply surprised and baffled them and they went away (Matt. 22:15-21).

The Sadducees, who said there is no resurrection, also tried to corner Jesus with a question about seven brothers (Matt. 22:23-33). When the first man died, leaving his wife and no children to carry on his name, the second brother married the woman. When he died, the third married her and so on until all were dead and there were no children. Then the woman died. The Sadducees asked Jesus, "In the resurrection, whose wife will she be, for she had been the wife of each of them?"

Jesus replied, "Your trouble is that you don't know the

Scriptures, and don't know the power of God. For when these seven brothers and the woman rise from the dead, they won't be married—they will be like angels."

When you find yourself trapped in what appears to be an either/or situation, look for a creative solution. Ask the Holy Spirit to help you and to direct you to whatever research may be appropriate. Sometimes you will be amazed and delighted at his answers.

God gave one wife an unusual solution after a ten-year battle over what to deduct on the income tax. She mentioned, "There's a guy in our church who specializes in preparing taxes." And to her surprise, her husband agreed to see the accountant. Now there's a third person both she and her husband trust, an "authority" to tell her husband what he can and can't do.

## WE ARE NOT OUR HUSBAND'S TEACHER

Both teaching our husbands and convicting them of sin are responsibilities of the Holy Spirit. Our role is to be honest with our husbands about how their behavior affects us. And we can pray. We can do no more, and we should do no less.

Some of us try to intervene because we hate for our husbands to look foolish. But be honest. We are also concerned for our own reputation, how his actions reflect back on us.

That is a trap—tying your self-worth to your husband's behavior. Try to separate yourself from what he does. You are two different people. You don't need to be embarrassed by his behavior. He alone is responsible for it. And ultimately, both of you are accountable individually to God for what you do.

God has not called us to control our husbands or change their conduct. If we try to force them to change they will resent it, even lash back at us and probably intensify the very behavior that upsets us. This leaves us frustrated, hurt, and our communication, our intimacy, our whole relationship suffers.

## BE BLAMELESS

He may be testing. Many men will try to get their wives to waver in their convictions, to back down. But remember, your husband loves you partly because of your purity, because you are a "sweet fragrance." It is possible he is testing to see if you really believe what you say and he would be disappointed if you compromised your values.

Stand for what you believe. This doesn't mean that, in making your stand, you are accountable for changing his mind or getting him to see things your way. It means that you personally uphold what you believe is right so that Jesus will find you blameless when he returns (2 Pet. 3:14).

God may use your stand to protect your husband. On their income tax return, Phyllis's husband listed charitable deductions far above what they had actually given. Phyllis refused to sign. After a heated battle, her husband begrudgingly relented. Two years later, the IRS audited their return and would likely have found the illegal claims.

## WE ARE NOT OF THE WORLD

Jesus has sent us into the world, but we are not a part of the world. We won't fit into the world's mold (John 17:14-16).

Jesus was not of the world, either. Because of this, he was never afraid of being tempted by it or being sucked into its evil. He felt free to go any place, with anyone. He came to save sinners, not to encourage the self-righteous. We too need to go where the sinners are, because as Christians we are commanded to let our light shine before men (Matt. 5:16).

So we both attend our husbands' company parties and have found unexpected dividends in going. Sometimes we have met people to whom we could witness. ("Is that a Christian fish you're wearing around your neck?" was the opener for Bev at one corporate banquet.) And if Bev hadn't been at one cocktail party, she would never have been able to share the Lord with a man whose mother was dying.

Moreover, both of us have benefited from seeing our husbands through coworkers' eyes. How else would we have learned of the special kindnesses our husbands do for the men in their department, or of the esteem in which they are held by their subordinates and bosses?

## WE ARE NOT TO JUDGE OUR HUSBANDS

It is so easy to develop a spiritual superiority complex, to lapse into a holier-than-he mode! As one wife confessed, "It seems I'm always wearing the white hat—the good guy in our family. And most of the time my husband is cast as the bad guy in the black hat." We may even think we are better than he. But we're wrong.

When "better than" feelings creep into your life, remember, "All have sinned and fall short of the glory of God" (Rom. 3:23). That includes you as well as your husband.

God has a way of reminding us of this from time to time. Several women mentioned occasions when their husbands' ethics proved more "Christian" than their own. "I don't want to put mother in a nursing home, but it would change our whole life-style if she were to move in with us," Marcia pondered. "If you are going to honor her," replied her unbelieving husband, "you will bring her here. It's OK with me."

## BLESSED ARE THE PEACEMAKERS

There will be situations where you can compromise. Be a peacemaker and take advantage of them. Don't feel that you are copping out, but do be sure to pray each dilemma through before making a decision. If, after you decide to compromise, the issue continues to nag and eat away at you, you can revise your assessment.

Giving is a compromise in many families. Kerry, who had been a bookkeeper, handled all the checks in her household and decided to tithe without asking her husband. She continued contributing to her church even when her husband was out of work. "We had holey underwear," she laughs, "but we made it."

However, at tax time her husband "went through the roof" when he saw how much she had given. When he had calmed down, instead of assuming defeat, she asked, "Well, what would you be willing to give?" He named an amount much smaller than what she had been tithing, but she was elated; he was giving for the first time.

## GOD SPEAKS TO UNBELIEVERS, TOO

As a believer, you also run the risk of feeling you alone have a direct pipeline to God for learning what is best for your household. But be careful. Paul urged you to "accept him whose faith is weak, without passing judgment on disputable matters" (Rom. 14:1). And God showed Nebuchadnezzar, king of Babylon, what to do when he was an unbeliever. Surely God can also guide your husband. So don't take over all decision making in your family in the belief that you alone can receive from God. When you pray for direction for the two of you, ask God to show your husband his will for you both.

This is what Patty did when she felt a deep need to bring an alcoholic sister into her home for rehabilitation. "It meant her coming with her three kids, too," Patty recalled. "It seemed to me this was her only hope, but my husband was terribly busy at work and not at all ready to take on four extra people in the house. I prayed that the Lord would show him what we should do, and he finally suggested that we should rent the place next door for them."

## COUNT THE COST

Saying no in many areas of your marriage may be "no biggie" to you or your husband. But there may be some issues about which your husband feels adamant. If you oppose him there, you must face the fact that you may endanger the warmth in your relationship, and possibly the marriage itself.

After Jesus explained the cost of following him, he gave this admonition: "Suppose one of you wants to build a tower. Will he not first sit down and estimate the cost to see if he has enough money to complete it? For if he lays the foundation and is not able to finish it, everyone who sees it will ridicule him, saying, 'This fellow began to build and was not able to finish'" (Luke 14:28-30).

Count the cost when you consider confronting your husband on issues that are important to him. You can never take back words once said, and it is extremely difficult to undo the anger they may generate.

## BUT HE INSISTS, AND I CAN'T LIVE WITH IT

What happens when your husband is immovable about those bottom line problems that are so damaging to you, to your children, to your marriage, that you cannot live with them? Which issues are that serious? They will be different for each person, and must be worked out between you and the Lord. For us, they include wife swapping, adultery, and violent abuse of our children or of us.

These issues endanger the marriage so severely that we feel we would have nothing to lose and perhaps everything to gain by taking a stand. But how should we make that stand?

Michelle McCormick, Ph.D., psychologist with CORE, a Christian counseling center in Newport Beach, California, suggests the following steps:

*Confrontation.* This is biblical. Jesus said, "If a brother sins against you, go and show him his fault, just between the two of you. If he listens to you, you have won your brother over" (Matt. 18:15).

If a woman has been verbally or emotionally tyrannized

by her husband, it can be frightening, but sometimes her response is exactly what the husband wanted to accomplish. "H'ray," one husband responded when confronted about swearing at the children. "You're finally getting some backbone!"

Still you may need some "courage pills" in the form of reinforcement from friends, family, a support group, or even a counselor.

*Then, plan your approach carefully.* If your husband tends to overpower you verbally, you may even have to memorize what you want to say. Pick your time carefully. Review our suggestions for improving communications mentioned in an earlier chapter.

When you are alone together and have his undivided attention, use "I" messages, such as "I feel angry/bitter/afraid/sad when you treat me/the children this way." Or, "It worries me how it affects the children when you . . ." Or, "I don't like it when you . . . It makes me feel . . ." Follow your "I" statement with, "We need to do something about this."

The Bible gives us a beautiful example of the confrontation of an unbelieving husband by a wife who knew the risks and worked hard to prepare her husband so he would hear her. Esther, the courageous Jewish woman who became queen of the Medo-Persian empire, risked her life to approach King Xerxes, for it was against the law for her to go unless he summoned her. Her mission was to ask the king to spare her people. She moved very cautiously and carefully. But first, she fasted and prayed.

When the king asked what she wanted and offered her even half his kingdom, she insisted upon inviting him to a banquet, and then invited him back the second night. Only after he felt honored and respected by her attention (and well-fed, too) did she make her request.

Ideally, of course, after you talk with your husband he will recognize the problem and suggest a solution. But it may take him some time to absorb what you have said. So give it space, and pray for a change.

If you see no change, go on to plan B:

*Go back with a friend.* If there is someone whose advice your husband respects, talk to him and see if he will go with you to talk with your husband. Christ's statement in Matthew 18 continued: "But if he will not listen, take one or two others along" (v. 16).

But be careful here. The biblical instructions are for Christian brothers who, it is assumed, are willing to be obedient to the Word. Your husband may resent a third person interfering in his marriage. In fact, we know some men who would be furious.

If you decide to take this step, your goal is not to embarrass or to pull a power play, but to get a feel for whether or not your husband is willing to work on the situation. You must make it clear that you want to look at your part in the problem through someone who can be objective—a support group, the counsel of women who know you well, or perhaps even a professional counselor.

*If still there is no change, take the next step.* Tell him the situation remains unbearable for you. Ask that he see a counselor or therapist with you. This should not be stated as a threat.

It should be a realistic statement of the situation as you see it. It would be a good idea to do your homework beforehand, so you can suggest specific help—a pastor, member of the counseling staff of a large church, marriage counselor, or psychologist in private practice.

If he isn't willing, go yourself, if it is at all possible. At least you may get some help in coping.

Then if there is no change and if he does not recognize the validity of your distress, you can take one more step.

*Time out.* This usually means asking your husband to leave for a period of time, with the goal being reconciliation. If he refuses to leave, you may have to move out. Remember, this is time out, not divorce, and during this period, all efforts should be directed toward getting back together again in an emotionally and physically healthy and safe environment. Ideally during this time you and your husband will agree to meet once weekly with a therapist or pastor.

Often, this period apart brings problem areas to the surface and provides objectivity in dealing with them. And, in the words of therapist Michelle McCormick, "It really works!"

Time out is often the only answer for husbands who habitually become abusive, for they are impulsive, out of control.

Unfortunately, we must recognize that some men will not submit to counseling even if it means losing their marriage. So, again we say, count the cost before you go this far.

## WHAT MAKES THE RULES WORK?

As we struggle to absorb this chapter, remember that if we take the whole Word of God, we find God's love and mercy covering the rules. He loved us while we were yet sinners, and he loves our husbands. We need to learn to love our husbands even though we don't approve of all their behavior. So all these principles must always be tempered with consideration of what is loving, what is caring—for us, for our husbands, and for others.

## THE FREEDOM OF FORGIVENESS

We have done everything. We have tried everything. We are hurt, frustrated, angry. He won't change. And nothing can change the past—the damage that has been done.

Stacy was appalled when her son, a high school senior, revealed the extent of his sexual promiscuity. She felt helpless during his college years as the girls came and went and he finally settled briefly with Michelle, who had had two abortions. Stacy grew to love Michelle and suffered with her and her son when Michelle found she was pregnant again. The ultimate solution—another abortion—broke Stacy's heart.

Stacy forgave her son and Michelle, but it was years later in a Bible study that she realized she blamed this whole devastating chain of events on her husband, who had passed on his free and easy sexual values to their son. When she forgave her husband, she experienced a release of bitterness she hadn't even known was there. "Although the sense of freedom was tremendous," Stacy noted, "I find I have to re-forgive my husband each time my son takes a new lover."

Forgiveness isn't easy. It isn't simple. It often takes time. It requires a trust in God. It doesn't make our husbands right or make the circumstances all wonderful. But it frees us from bitterness, from blaming, from the bondage of anger. Most important, forgiveness sets us free to love again!

## QUESTIONS FOR FURTHER STUDY AND GROUP DISCUSSION

A word of caution: Your small group by now, one might hope, has become a warm, safe place for honest sharing, but during this session you may need to be careful about revealing information that would embarrass your husband.

1. Which "Common Problem Areas" mentioned in the chapter do you and your husband struggle with? Which differences are biblical and which are cultural—that is, learned from your parents or other authority figures in your life? Note the areas you feel free to share in your group.

2. Which scriptural principles in the chapter do you already use to help you decide what is right in situations of conflict? Were any new to you? Which are the most difficult for you to apply? Are there any you did not understand?

3. Read the Book of Esther. She is one of the clearest examples we have in Scripture of a believing wife married to an unbeliever. (Nabal and Abigail might be another to consider; see 1 Samuel 25.) Note how carefully she approached

her husband. What principles could you apply to your relationship with your husband?

4. Have you and your husband had value differences that you have resolved successfully? Are there any that you can share with your group without casting your husband as "the bad guy"?

5. Sometimes, no matter what we do or say, we still have painful differences in our marriages. What are you doing to cope in those situations? What scriptural principles are especially helpful?

6. How does your husband express his disappointment or anger when you do stand firm or feel you must say no to him? How do you respond to him? Do you have any ways of protecting yourself emotionally from his anger? Consider these verses:

> *Ephesians 6:13-19*
> *James 4:6-8*

7. How do you handle your negative feelings—the anger, frustration, hurt, disappointment, helplessness, self-pity—that come when you can not resolve a difference comfortably for both of you?

> *James 5:16*
> *1 John 1:9*
> *Matthew 5:22-24, 6:12-15, 7:1-5*

**Pray that God will give your husband a hunger for godliness and that he will help you be honest and forgiving.**

# EIGHT
# WHEN THE PROBLEMS ARE INSURMOUNTABLE

This is the chapter we didn't want to write, because it departs so markedly from our theme of learning to be a contented wife. But the more we researched, the more convinced we became that we must address the hard truths of problems far above and beyond living with a husband who simply doesn't believe as we believe, or even the husband who is "difficult." We are talking about abuse—repeated, severe abuse.

Millions of women throughout this country live with abuse. Every eighteen seconds, according to one survey, a woman is battered by a husband or boyfriend.[1] Countless others are abused in less visible but equally damaging ways. We urge you, even if you feel this material doesn't apply to you, to familiarize yourself with this "private crime." Since some estimate that 50 percent of women experience some level of abuse,[2] we all need to understand it and to learn how to help.

The abusive husband may assault his wife emotionally, leaving deep psychological scars. He may batter her physically. Or he may abuse her sexually. He may attack the children. He may be a tyrant, an alcoholic, a drug addict, a compulsive gambler, or a failure as a provider.

It is particularly difficult for the Christian wife with an

unbelieving husband to deal with such a situation. After all, she has heard again and again that she must be a submissive wife, that she must persevere under trial, that she may win her husband "without a word." She is told, too, that she must get rid of all bitterness, rage, and anger; forgive as, in Christ, God forgives her, and that she must never, never divorce.

And so, often without even the neighbors or friends knowing, innumerable women live in desperation. They hurt terribly—emotionally or physically or both. They are ashamed, frightened, furious. But most of all, they feel helpless, trapped, or, as one woman expressed it, "I guess I'm condemned to hell."

The wife of an unbelieving or barely believing husband may fantasize that if he would just become a committed Christian, everything would change. Unfortunately, this often is not true. Evangelical Christian counselor James Alsdurf points out that wife abuse can be found in virtually every church.[3]

Alsdurf also quoted a study by Straus-Steinmetz and Gelles revealing that a woman who marries a man of a different religion is almost twice as likely to be hit by her husband as a woman who marries someone of the same faith. He further stated, "Husbands without religious preference are more likely to use violence on their wives."

## WHAT IS ABUSE?

Often a woman is so isolated, she doesn't recognize that her husband's behavior is outside the norm. Here are some questions developed from interviews with those who work with abuse that will help you determine if you are abused:[4]

1. Does your husband attack your self-esteem or that of the children? ("You can't do anything right." "You're such rotten kids.")

2. Are you or the children always blamed for his anger? ("If you weren't so sloppy, I wouldn't get so mad.")

3. Does he want to control you? Does he control all the money, check the mileage on the car, keep you from going to church, read your mail? Is he jealous of your relationships outside the home?

4. Is he a poor provider? Does he have trouble holding a job, manage money badly, gamble, keep you in debt, and blame you, though the problems are obviously his fault?

5. Is there substance abuse—alcohol or drugs? Does it cause blackouts, memory loss, drunk driving arrests, lost work days, lost weekends, embarrassing or frightening incidents?

6. Are you or the children afraid of him? Do you feel like you are walking on eggs, that you forever must edit everything you say? Are you fearful of emotional or physical reprisals?

7. Must you continually sacrifice your needs and wishes and those of the children to keep peace?

8. Is the situation so frightening you feel you must lie to him or others to keep him from getting angry?

9. Has he attacked you physically (pushing, slapping, kicking, hitting) or sexually more than once?

10. Are you afraid he might seriously injure or kill you or the children? When he threatens, do you sense he could really follow through?

All of these are abusive situations and need to be faced with specific steps working toward change. But there is still more to understand.


## THE PATTERN OF AN ABUSIVE RELATIONSHIP

Those who work with wife abuse find there is a predictable pattern. Abuse tends to follow a three-phase cycle. It begins with the "buildup," when the tension mounts and the man becomes picky, nervous, tense. Next comes the "episode of violence," which may include verbal tirades or physical and sexual battering. Last (but not always) the husband becomes remorseful, or at least temporarily calm. He may bring flowers and shower his wife with concern and attention. Over the years, this "honeymoon period" tends to become shorter or to cease, while the violence intensifies.

Alcohol or drugs are often involved. Some men end their abuse when they get help to stop their drinking, but many do not.

From interviews with personnel at shelters for abused women and from data gathered by Lenore E. Walker in her book, *The Battered Woman,*[5] these profiles of the partners in an abusive relationship emerge.

*Profile of an abusive husband.* He frequently comes from an abusive home, has low self-esteem, believes in male supremacy, blames others for his actions. He is childish, does things to excess (battering, spending, even buying gifts for her), but is possessive and jealous. He often presents a dual personality—both charming and cruel, selfish and generous, macho but fearful his woman will leave him. He has little tolerance for stress, uses sex as an act of aggression, and doesn't believe his violence should have negative consequences. His violence increases when his self-esteem is threatened—by trouble at work, when his wife's income or education surpasses his, when he fails as a provider.

The batterer is frequently described as an out-of-control person, but in fact, he does have a degree of control. He rarely abuses his wife in front of others and may become skilled at violence that doesn't show, such as choking or beating parts of the body normally covered by clothes.

*Portrait of an abused wife.* The woman holds traditional values regarding the home, marriage, and family. She usually did not experience violence in her home as a child and it was not evident in the courtship, when her man made her feel loved, special. So she was shocked the first time abuse occurred (often during her first pregnancy). She may have been a victim in other ways (rape, death of a parent, molestation, alcoholic parent) and struggles with low self-esteem. She believes she is responsible for her husband's violence, feels guilt and shame, yet denies her terror and anger.

Because she seems to do little to help herself, she appears passive but, in fact, she has great strength and works very hard to keep peace in her home and just to survive. She comes to believe no one can help her because her husband is so powerful, almost omnipotent. But she is not masochistic ("asks for it" or likes it), nor mentally unbalanced. She comes from every racial, educational, and economic background.

## WHY DOES SHE STAY?

Many of us wonder why a wife would stay in such a destructive situation. We become frustrated trying to help, because no matter how hard we try, she has a reason why she can't act to change the situation.

We don't understand that her fear and low self-esteem render her helpless, immobile, dependent on the relationship. (Actually, the husband is dependent on her, too, panicked at the thought of losing her.) We don't understand the coping mechanisms she develops in order to survive.

A woman often must deny, even to herself, that she is abused. As one counselor pointed out, it is easier to deny the facts, because once a woman admits them, she really has to do something about them. And doing something—particularly leaving and facing the unknown—is to her more terrifying than the known, no matter how miserable it may be. Here are some ways she thinks that keep her from leaving:

1. I'm worthless. Therefore I can't function on my own. And possibly, I deserve this treatment.
2. It's all my fault. I need to try harder. If I were more spiritual, it would all work out.
3. Without a man, without my marriage, I'd be only half a person.
4. I couldn't make it financially on my own. I haven't any skills, talents. We would live in poverty. I have no resources.
5. It isn't really such a problem. He loses his temper, but he is not an abuser. He gets drunk, but he isn't an alcoholic;

after all, he goes to work most mornings. He went three whole weeks without gambling.

6. It is going to get better when his promotion comes through or when the kids are older. He has promised he'll stop.

7. I love him. And he can be so loving, so generous, so sorry for what he has done.

8. I feel responsible for him. I might be the one to help him be saved. I can help him to change. Who else understands him?

9. It is better for the children to have a father, even an abusive one, than no father at all. Separation would be traumatic for them.

10. He says if I leave I won't get a penny from him, or he'll come after me, kill me/steal the children/hurt my family.

11. I'm too frightened to do anything when he is abusive and it seems pointless when he is being nice.

12. Nobody would believe me. His friends, coworkers, think he is wonderful. It would be my word against his.

13. The Bible forbids divorce and I just have to stick it out.

These attitudes keep her trapped. But we need to persevere in extending lifelines to her, again and again. Because the bottom line, according to all the experts in abuse whom we have interviewed—Christian and non-Christian—is that separation is essential if a woman and her children are in danger. And, except that God would give her a miracle, it is her only hope of getting her husband to cease his violence.

## IS THIS YOU?

Do you see yourself and your husband in some of what we describe? Any abuse damages love and should be taken seriously. But perhaps the abuse in your marriage is occasional and mild and neither you nor your children feel afraid. Then prayer and the techniques we discussed in previous chapters—seeking to build your husband's self-esteem by meeting his deep needs as a man, and using assertive communicative skills to express your feelings and needs—may help to work toward change.

However, if you feel you or your children may be in danger, you are way, way past the point of confronting, communicating, even beyond simply praying and standing in faith for your marriage. This is the time to listen to James who wrote, "Faith without works is dead." Pray for God's guidance, trust the Lord, and act.

Get yourself and your children away from your husband to a safe place. Separation makes a strong statement to your husband that there must be a change. And Linda Russell of Life Dimensions, a Christian counseling center in Los Alamitos, California, emphasized, "It is almost impossible to effect a change if the couple remains together."

## SEPARATION IS NOT DIVORCE

Many women refuse to leave because they equate separation with divorce. Leaving does not mean you want or plan to divorce. Ms. Russell suggests that your goal is twofold: to be safe and to work on your marriage with the intent of saving it.

We are called by God to suffer for our faith. If your suffering would bring your husband to Christ, it might be worth risking the danger of staying. But those who work with wife abuse say that just doesn't happen. Separation and getting help for yourself is your best hope to help your husband change. It will confront him with his sin and give him a compelling reason to deal with it.

Statistically, we know his abuse will probably escalate if it is not checked. He is like the "evil men" of whom Paul wrote who "go from bad to worse" (2 Tim. 3:13). You are not your husband's helper, as God called you to be, if you submit to abuse and allow it to continue.

And most important, even if you have reached the point of not caring about yourself, you must protect your children. If you don't intervene, your sons are likely to grow into abusive men, repeating the sins of their father. And your children may lose respect for you because you were too weak to protect yourself and them. Remember, too, if the authorities find one of your children is abused physically or sexually, and you made no effort to protect him, you could be charged with neglect and all your children could be taken by the court and placed in foster care.

Leaving is never easy, and you should be aware that many husbands promise to change, beg their wives to return, make terrifying threats. They will do anything to get their wives back under their control. Others simply go find another woman, and a few commit suicide. No matter how your husband reacts, you must remember you are not responsible for his behavior, and you still must seek safety for yourself and your children.

## THE BIBLE SAYS . . .

But, you say, this isn't scriptural? Isn't it?

Do you believe abuse is a sin? Surely it grieves God's heart. Paul wrote that we are not to "associate with immoral men; not at all meaning the immoral of this world, or the greedy and robbers, or idolaters, since then you would need to go out of the world. But rather I wrote to you not to associate with anyone who bears the name of brother if he is guilty of immorality or greed, or is an idolater, reviler, drunkard, or robber—not even to eat with such a one" (I Cor. 5:9-11, RSV). Abusive behavior, then, was considered as serious as sexual immorality or idol worship!

Later Paul listed those who will not inherit the kingdom of God, including fornicators, idolaters, adulterers . . . thieves, drunkards, and revilers. (1 Cor. 6:9-10). *Strong's Exhaustive Concordance* gives the Greek word for revilers as *loidoros,* the same Greek word that is translated "abusive" in the previous passage (1 Cor. 5).[6]

Abuse actually goes against the whole of the gospel. The

woman who remains under the cruel tyranny of her husband—a blind doormat of subservience—is held in bondage by legalism. (Submit to thy husband, no matter what! Thou shalt never, no never, divorce!) But Jesus died to bring us love, mercy, grace, to set us free from unbiblical enslavement. Jesus esteemed women and treated them with honor and respect.

Those who get so stuck on the word *submissive* in 1 Peter 3 may fail to read on to verse 6. Pointing to Sarah as our example, Peter concluded, "You are her daughters if you do what is right and do not give way to fear."

Remember, too, never in the Bible is anyone given permission to dominate us or to force us into submission. God doesn't even do that. Submission is to be given willingly, not out of fear or physical coercion.

The Bible gives us, in Abigail, an excellent example of a woman who took specific steps to do what was right when her spouse placed her and her family in danger (1 Sam. 25). Her husband, Nabal, was described as "surly, mean, and wicked." David, who had protected Nabal's shepherds in the wilderness, asked Nabal for provisions. When Nabal refused, David was furious, took his sword, and gathered his men to attack.

But Abigail, warned of the impending disaster, went to meet David with bread, wine, sheep, grain, and cakes, without telling her husband. Recognizing her husband's sin, she responded courageously to do what was right to protect her family and herself.

The abused woman, then, it seems to us, is following a biblical precedent when she takes a stand against the sin of abuse in her home, accepting her responsibility before the Lord to do what is right.

## SEEK WISE COUNSEL

Whether you are ready to leave yet or not, you need wise counsel. Don't settle for advice from a person who cannot be objective, from someone who feels a husband's violence is always the wife's fault.

Most Christians talk first with their pastors, but your pastor can't be an expert in everything. Don't be afraid to ask him to recommend someone with specific training and experience in helping those in domestic violence (and substance addiction, if that is part of the problem).

Crisis hot lines often offer telephone counseling or may give you a referral. Some women's shelters give free counseling to help you explore your options. Check the white or yellow pages of your telephone book under "Crisis Intervention" or "Women's Services and Organizations" for hot lines and shelters.

You may feel more comfortable (and get better faster) working with a woman. It is often difficult for a man to understand the woman's point of view in an abusive situation, and it will be easier for you to tell a woman everything. Many abused women tell only a little of what is happening because it is so embarrassing. Your counselor needs to know it all.

You may also want to read some books on abuse, such as Holly Wagner Green's *Turning Fear to Hope* (Thomas Nelson) or *No Place to Hide* by Esther Lee Olson with Kenneth Petersen (Tyndale House) to help you understand your problems and your options more clearly.

## LEGAL ADVICE

You will need to know your legal rights. Again, your crisis hot line may be able to offer you counsel. Some attorneys will give you one consultation free. And shelters for abused women usually can give you information.

See if your state offers a booklet such as *The Legal Rights of Battered Women in California.* This is a clear and straightforward what-to-do handbook that explains such essentials as calling the police, pressing charges, what you can legally take if you move out. The library or local bar association or even your police department may be able to help you with such information. It is particularly important that you understand your legal rights regarding the children, so your actions can't be construed as kidnapping.

Also, you would be wise to start collecting evidence of your abuse. You may need it later if you have to go to court. Ask a friend to take photographs of your bruises, get copies of police and hospital reports, or at least make a note of the dates, so they can be retrieved later. You may want to keep a diary. If you can't keep it safely at home, you could mail notes to a relative or friend to save for you.

At the end of this chapter is a list of things you will need to start a new life. Gather them together in a safe place, so you can get them quickly if you need to leave in a hurry.

## WHEN AND HOW TO LEAVE

*The timing.* A rule of thumb suggested by Esther Lee Olson and Kenneth Petersen in their case study of an abused wife, *No Place to Hide*[7] is that the wife should leave the home if abuse occurs a third time. This, they point out, constitutes a pattern of abuse.

The easiest time to leave is as soon as you are physically able after a bout of abuse, when you are most angry and your husband is usually calmer and less on guard.

*Finding a safe place.* Where will you go? Look for a place where you will be safe, where your husband either can't find you or would be afraid to abuse you. Perhaps you have family members or a friend who will take you in. However, consider their safety, as well as your own, for some husbands are so enraged, they come looking for their wives, ready to kill. If your husband is extremely volatile, you may want to ask people who care about you to suggest a place he won't find, perhaps with a more distant relative or a friend your husband doesn't know.

If this isn't feasible, you need information on the shelters available to you. Your church may be able to refer you, or

149

look again in the telephone book under "Crisis Intervention" for hot lines or "Women's Services and Organizations." Or call your local hospital or police department and ask who helps abused wives in your area. You needn't give your name. Your county or city departments of family services, social services, health and welfare also may refer you to help. Generally you will receive only a phone number. Shelter locations are often kept secret to protect their clients.

Some shelters may be full and have waiting lists. But in certain areas emergency programs offer immediate shelter in motel rooms for a few days, until women can find another place. Some shelters take only the most severe cases. Most offer only shared rooms. But many will give you counseling over the phone, helping you explore your options. If you and the shelter personnel decide the shelter is for you, you will usually be met in some neutral place, and they may request that you not disclose your location to anyone.

There are some 900 such shelters throughout the country where you will find safe refuge. In most cases, you will also participate in an intensive counseling program to help restore your self-esteem and gain back your independence. They may assist you in applying for welfare and possibly starting a job training program. Usually you will have an opportunity to participate in group sessions to explore goals for the future and to talk through common problems with other women at the shelter. Many shelters also offer referrals for your husband to groups where he can learn to control or eliminate abusive behavior.

Unfortunately, it is not easy today to find a Christian shelter, although a few exist. Some are run by coalitions of churches. We are praying that God will raise up more in coming years.

## GETTING A RESTRAINING ORDER
Often the shelter personnel or crises centers can help you protect yourself and your children by applying for a

restraining order from the court against your husband. The judge's order can cover such details as how far away your husband must stay from you or the children, your temporary custody of the children, use of the car and house. You can also ask that your husband be ordered to pay certain bills and to provide child support. If he fails to comply, he can be arrested.

You do not need witnesses to obtain a restraining order. Procedures may vary in different states but generally, on the basis of your written application describing the abuse, the judge will issue a temporary, then a permanent, restraining order. The permanent order is good for a year and may be extended if you need more time. Even if you think your husband will not respect the order, be sure to get it. Surprisingly, many abusive husbands do abide by it when they understand they can be arrested for violation.

## HELP FOR HUSBANDS

The sad statistics are that very few men who beat their wives change. (Counselors told us less than one percent.) Often, they refuse counseling or therapy, denying any responsibility, claiming, "She drove me to it."

In a survey, Maureen Pirog-Good, a researcher with the school of public and environmental affairs at Indiana University, found 103 organizations that help men with their anger. Many deal primarily with referrals from the criminal justice system. She learned that, on the average, of every 100 men who enroll in these programs, sixty will eventually complete them. And of those, forty-two to fifty-three will not return to battering within a year.

However, according to Kathleen Carlin, former director of a women's shelter who now serves as director of Men Stopping Violence, probably only two-tenths of one percent of abusive men will ever make it into such a group. Still, she insists that if a man really wants to change and is willing to work on it, he can.[8]

It seems there is much still to learn about helping these men. But new programs continue to develop around the country, including those based on mandatory arrest of abusive husbands, with the police, not the victim, pressing charges.[9] We pray that in the next few years treatment will become more effective and more men will see its value.

## TAKE YOUR TIME

Don't leap into making any permanent decisions. You need time to heal and grow after you leave a dangerous situation—usually months, not just days or weeks. And give your husband plenty of time to seek help. Avoid the temptation, generated by loneliness or insecurity, to return to him until he is seeking help and there is clear evidence that his behavior has changed. Many men fake change, so be very cautious. Again, pray, seeking God's will and get wise counsel, both spiritual and legal, from those who know your situation intimately.

If your husband refuses help and shows no evidence of change, you may need to think about making your separation permanent with divorce. Please take your time and consider carefully the Scripture and the doctrines of your church. Most Christians consider adultery grounds for divorce (Matt. 19:9). And according to Paul's advice, when the unbelieving partner leaves, you are not under bondage (1 Cor. 7:15).

But we feel that the extremely abusive husband has already broken the marriage by failing to love his wife as he loves his own body, as he is instructed (Eph. 5:28-29). He repeatedly injures rather than protects his wife. It seems to us that he loves himself and his own lusts in the place of his wife and family. It is as though he is having a love affair with himself, no matter how costly it may be to others. He has become his own idol. And one of the dictionary definitions of adultery is idolatry.

Often in the church we hear teaching that implies no one

should ever get a divorce. Yet when Malachi 2:14–16 states that God hates divorce, it is clear that God is speaking to the husbands and is angry with the men who have dealt treacherously with their wives, forcing them into divorce.

Some suggest that the Christian wife should wait and let her husband file for divorce. Unfortunately abusive men seldom initiate divorce. They feel they own their wives and refuse to relinquish control. An abused wife often has waited too long already for her husband to change, for someone to rescue her. Now she needs to prayerfully decide what is best for her and her children and move forward with courageous faith.

Those who still feel divorce is not appropriate for them may want to look into a legal separation which, in many states, will provide permanent arrangements for child custody and support.

## "BUT I JUST CAN'T"

If you are an abused wife, the material we have presented may seem overwhelming to you. You may feel utterly unable to take any of the steps we have outlined. Don't let this create more guilt or feelings of worthlessness. We think you are special to be able to survive in such a situation, and we know you are making the best decisions you can. But please, reread this chapter. Don't throw away the ideas we have given you. It may take months or even years, but one day some part of our suggestions may be exactly right for you.

## YOUR NEW LIFE

It is not easy to start over again, either financially or emotionally. But many women experience such a sense of release after they leave an abusive situation that they wonder why they didn't do it long ago. You will find that you are stronger than you think, and although it may be tough in the beginning, you have the assurance that you are right with God and that he will see you through.

There are many promises of God's care in the Bible. One that has been very meaningful to us is from Isaiah: "See, I am doing a new thing! Now it springs up; do you not perceive it? I am making a way in the desert and streams in the wasteland" (3:19).

If you anticipate leaving, try to assemble specific items which may be difficult for you to retrieve later. These include:

> Identification for yourself
> Driver's license
> Birth certificates—yours and your children's
> Money
> Ownership papers for the car
> House deed
> Check books
> Bank books
>   (or at least account numbers and bank location)
> Credit cards
> Insurance papers
> Keys
> Medications
> Child's favorite toy or blanket
> Medical records for each family member
> Social security card
> Welfare identification
> School records
> Work permits
> Green card, if you are an immigrant
> Passport
> Marriage license
> Jewelry
> Small saleable objects
> Address book
> Pictures

## QUESTIONS FOR FURTHER STUDY
## AND GROUP DISCUSSION

1. In the chapter we mention that abuse goes against the whole of the gospel. Gospel means "good news." What is the "good news" of the Bible? Below are some Scriptures to start you thinking. Add others of your own. Do you agree with the application in the chapter that Jesus came to set an abused wife free?

> *Matthew 11:28-30*
> *John 3:16-17*
> *John 8:32*
> *Romans 7:6*
> *Romans 8:1-2*
> *1 John 1:9*

2. The Bible says we are to rejoice when we share the sufferings of Christ. What are the sufferings of Christ? How do you share in those sufferings? What part of suffering in a difficult marriage is suffering for Christ? Consider the following verses before you try to answer these questions.

> *Matthew 5:10-12*
> *Romans 8:16-18*
> *Philippians 1:27-30*
> *Hebrews 2:10*
> *1 Peter 4:12-16*

3. Read Abigail's story in *1 Samuel 25.* Do you think she did the right thing? Was she a helper to her husband? A submissive wife? Does the Bible express any disapproval of her actions?

4. Read *Acts 4:34-5:11.* Do you think Sapphira was a submissive wife? Was God pleased with her actions?

5. Discuss again what it is like to be a doormat. Might Sap-

phira have been a doormat? How is biblical submission different?

6. Of course we would like to see an abusive marriage restored to health, but often the husband refuses to change. Read the following passages on divorce.

>*Malachi 2:13-16*
>*Matthew 5:31-32*
>*Matthew 19:3-11*
>*1 Corinthians 7:1-16*

How do you feel about this chapter's position on this issue? (Remember, we all don't have to agree. The church has struggled with this issue since the time of Christ, and ultimately we each have to make the best decision we can in our particular situation. We are grateful that God is merciful and has provided us with forgiveness.)

7. Most abused wives are afraid and ashamed. Therefore they say little of the horror they live in. If we suspect abuse, we need to ask direct questions. Reread "What Is Abuse?" and develop some questions to help a woman open up. What else can we do to help? What should we avoid doing? What help is available in your church and community for abused wives?

(Remember, an abused wife may be a dependent person looking for someone to make decisions for her. Encourage her to become independent. Keep asking her what she thinks. Be patient. She may leave her husband several times before she has the courage to stay away. And remember, the abusive husband can be extremely dangerous.)

**Pray together for protection, guidance, and courage for those women you know who might be in abusive marriages. Pray too for the healing of their husbands.**

# NINE
# SHARING THE LORD WITH OUR KIDS

Experts in child development repeatedly emphasize the importance of parents presenting to their children a united front on basic issues. But obviously, in a marriage with an unbelieving or barely believing husband, it is impossible for the two spouses to stand together in the area of faith. What, then, will happen to the children?

Or, as one young mother of a newborn and a two-year-old said, "Will they go his way—or mine? Obviously, I feel mine is the right way. But it's all so sensitive, so awkward, so uncomfortable!"

Often this discomfort is fed by what we hear at church:

"Of course you kids are bringing your parents to the Sunday school picnic." (Our children would love to bring Dad, but too often, he won't come.)

"All Christians should say grace at meals." (Grace isn't very effective if Dad, across the table, glares or makes cutting remarks.)

"The father is the spiritual leader of the home." (But what if he doesn't even believe in God?)

"My husband leads our family devotions and the children have grown so much." (Oh, how we yearn for that to happen in our homes, but should we just wait, hoping someday, by some miracle, it will?)

## LEADER OR PRIEST

As much as we long to lead our children to the Lord, to teach them about God, many of us feel concern about taking control, usurping our husband's roles. Is it right for us to assume leadership? Or is that really the issue? Do we have to take over the headship of the home to teach our children the things that are important to us?

Some Christians have taught that the husband is the priest of the home, but Scripture tells us as believers, "You are a chosen people, a royal priesthood, a holy nation, a people belonging to God, that you may declare the praises of him who called you out of darkness into his wonderful light" (1 Pet. 2:9).

Every Christian is a priest who can share the Lord. Why, then, couldn't and shouldn't you be a priest in your home—showing your children how God called you out of darkness into his wonderful light?

As you do this, however, do be watchful that your sharing never takes on a conspiratorial "us against Dad" coloring, but that it is rooted in a climate of love and respect for him, of "us for him."

And there is another danger here, warns psychologist Michele McCormick. The wife of the unbelieving or lukewarm Christian husband is lonely and wants desperately for the children to join her in Christ. So she needs to be careful that she is not "using" the child and trying to pull him or her into the faith, for this truly will backfire.


## SO HOW DO WE PASS ON OUR FAITH?

The really important values of life, the underlying principles by which we steer our lives, are often "caught" more than they are "taught." Children absorb our values and our beliefs as they live with us.

Dr. Laura A. Mathis, a licensed clinical psychologist with Associated Psychologists of Diamond Bar, California, says that where the parental values differ, children tend to adopt those of the parent with whom they most identify. This is the parent who takes time to feel with them, to listen to them, to encourage them, not the parent who nags, demands, or preaches.

## LIVING YOUR CHRISTIANITY BEFORE THEM

If our children are to "catch" our faith from living with our example, obviously the way we live the Christian life becomes all-important.

Does this mean being perfect? Of course not. That day won't come till we are in heaven. But we need to be growing Christians who are in Bible study, in fellowship with other Christians, and who have an intimate relationship in prayer with the Lord.

It is important that we be real—that we live and not just talk about what we believe. We need to allow our children to see our struggles as well as our victories, to honestly admit our mistakes as well as to share our answers to prayer, to seek their forgiveness as well as to teach them how to forgive.

One executive recalls, "When my mother overreacted, then sincerely asked my forgiveness, it made a huge impression. She was showing me that she wasn't perfect, but a person in whose life the Holy Spirit was working."

Living our Christianity doesn't mean we must do it like the pastor's wife or our Bible study teacher or like anyone else. God doesn't make carbon-copy Christians. We are each unique, with individual talents and weaknesses. Some rise early to spend time with the Lord; others don't come alive till noon. Some talk easily about their faith; others share only with difficulty.

No matter what our strengths or failings, there will be many times when we feel inadequate as Christian mothers. God doesn't expect us to be Super Mom, but to do what we can.

## PRAY FOR THEM

Of course you pray for your children. You pray from the very beginning of your Christian life. Perhaps you prayed even before the moment of your child's conception, if you were fortunate enough to know Christ then. Pray for your children's salvation, their growth in Christ, their safety, their friends, their eventual marriage partner, and all your other concerns for them.

Make God your partner in child rearing. He gave you these children—even if you didn't know him at the time. Ask him for the wisdom and strength to raise them to serve him.

It may help your children to realize how many times each day they are in your prayers. A man who had been a rebellious son told us he knew that no matter how outrageous his behavior, there was one thing he could not change: his mother's faithfulness in prayer for him.

## LOVE YOUR CHILDREN

It is vital for us to separate and clearly understand the difference between love, which is unconditional, and approval, which is always conditional and depends on performance. Rich Buehler, the wise talk show host of KBRT radio in Los Angeles, points out that God loves us unconditionally, but he doesn't always approve of us. Unconditional love is expressed in many ways: a hug or touch as you walk by, really listening when your child tells you of his day, a "Love ya and I'll be praying for you" as a child leaves to take a big test.

Approval, on the other hand, is praise for a good grade or a job well done; it is the trip to Disneyland for reading ten books during the summer. Approval used without an underlying foundation of unconditional love can apply too much pressure to perform and cause a backlash.

Moreover, love is essential in "discipling" your children. Here is how Dr. Ross Campbell, in *How to Really Love*

*Your Child,* explains it. "If a child does not feel loved and accepted, he has real difficulty identifying with his parents and their values." Without the strong, healthy love-bond, a child reacts to parental guidance with anger, resentment, and hostility.

Dr. Campbell continues, "To give a child the close relationship with God which they possess, parents must make sure a child feels unconditionally loved. Why? Because this is the way God loves us—unconditionally. It is extremely difficult for persons who do not feel unconditionally loved by their parents to feel loved by God."[1]

## DISCIPLINE OR TRAINING

We are commanded to train our children in the way they should go. But discipline can become a prickly issue between a husband and wife, and the division can grow even deeper when we are married to barely believing or unbelieving husbands. Many wives complain that their mates are too harsh with the children, and some that their husbands won't do any disciplining at all.

Joan was a teacher and believed that consistent discipline by both parents was essential. It distressed her that her style of discipline differed so much from that of her unbelieving husband. Her attempts to negotiate led to arguments, so she decided to see what would happen if he disciplined the kids in his way and she in hers. Her protective instincts were so strong that sometimes she had to leave the room to keep from interfering. She was surprised to find that her children had no difficulty in adjusting to two distinct styles of guidance.

Remember, even in marriages where both partners are Christians, parental strictness differs. Where possible, talk over your differences with your husband away from your children. But realize you will probably never come to perfect agreement. Unless your husband really abuses the children, your best bet will be to try to make your own discipline consistent with biblical teaching and to let God teach your husband.

The golden rule is a good guideline for biblical discipline: "Do to others as you would have them do to you" (Luke 6:31). None of us will adhere to this precept 100 percent of the time, but do try to think about how you would want to be disciplined before you endeavor to "train up" your children.

## DISCIPLINE BY GUILT?

Many of us have been brought up in homes where one technique of discipline was to make us feel guilty. "How could you do this to your poor mother?" "In my day, children never spoke back to their elders!" "You're just rotten clear through." Statements such as these are intended to shame us. They also undermine our self-esteem.

Making a child feel guilty may coerce a change in outward behavior, but it tends to create an angry, rebellious spirit, resistant not only to you, but to the things of God. Jesus taught, encouraged, invited. He was harsh only with those who refused to receive the truth, and even then, he did not exaggerate. He simply spoke the truth.

## DON'T CREATE ANGER IN YOUR CHILDREN

The Scriptures offer us a final guideline on discipline: "Fathers, do not exasperate your children; instead, bring them up in the training and instruction of the Lord" (Eph. 6:4).

Watch to see that your discipline does not "provoke wrath," as the King James Version expresses it. We are referring here not to a childish outburst that quickly passes, but a long-term seething fury that builds with each new incident.

Jill felt frustrated by increasing anger in her teenage son. Her simple requests provoked raging replies and any attempt at discipline threatened to develop into World War III. So Jill prayed and asked God to help her son to grow or to show her a better way of discipline. Then a neighbor commented that his wife disciplined by simply "calling" her children on their behavior without threats or punishment.

It was risky, but Jill decided to try it. She simply mentioned to her son that he was late to dinner. Or when he missed his curfew she told him she was worried. As she showed him more respect, as an adult interfacing with another adult, amazingly, his anger diminished and his behavior improved. He wasn't perfect, but now he tried and even apologized sometimes when he failed.

Our intentions are good. We want so badly for our children to become mature Christians that we may attempt to discipline them into Christianity. But forcing them into Christian conformity too often brings angry rebellion instead. There are no pat answers that work for every child, but as Christians we have the resource of an all-knowing God who, if we ask, can guide us in finding the best ways to discipline each of our children.

## COMMUNICATING THE CONCEPTS OF GOD

How much can a child really understand about God? Sometimes it is very frustrating, trying to explain Christian concepts to little ones who haven't the vocabulary or the experience necessary to understand. Still, there is much that they can understand.

*The first years.* Psychologist Michele McCormick told us that from birth to three and a half the child incorporates or identifies with the mother. Her warmth and love are extremely important.

These are the years, we find, when the child is learning that he or she is lovable, worthwhile as a person. This is essential if a youngster is to believe that God loves him.

*The middle years.* Then Dr. McCormick says the child begins emotional separation and individualization, and Dad becomes more important. This relationship becomes the child's stepping-stone to the world.

But we also see that mother continues to have influence because she normally spends more time with the children. These preschool and elementary school years, in fact, present great opportunities to the Christian mother. Her children are pliable, eager to learn, and readily accept what she shares. This is the time to reinforce the foundation of love already laid in her children's first years and to build on it.

There are so many ways to share over and over such basic Christian concepts as God loves us; God is good; God forgives us; we need to forgive others; the Bible is the Word of God; the Bible teaches us how to live; God has a special plan for our lives. Talk about these concepts in words your children understand, defining any religious terms.

When a child brings in a fuzzy caterpillar, mention that God created it or explain how God plans for it to become a butterfly. When your child makes a mistake and feels embarrassed, share that we all make mistakes, we're all sinners, but God still loves us just like Mommy still loves him.

Ask the Holy Spirit to show you opportunities and give you the words. Keep your statements short and simple, appropriate to your child's age, and stop before he loses interest. This doesn't come naturally or easily for most of us, but even seed sown only occasionally and in clumsiness can bear fruit. Remember, we are not in this alone. We have the extra edge of the Holy Spirit who takes that seed and will nourish it and bring it to maturity.

But don't put off sharing in the hope that it will be easier later. Pat remembers thinking that she would have plenty of time in the teen years to discuss some of the important aspects of Christianity with her kids: sex, dating, marriage, and total surrender to God. These subjects seemed too difficult for the elementary school years.

Unfortunately, when her children reached teen age, they had already picked up information on sex and dating from their peers and had little interest in Mom's ideas. How Pat wishes she had found ways to bring these values down to their level when they were younger and more open.

*The teen years.* Our children's teens are years of dramatic changes. As parents we experience bewilderment, surprise, pride, excitement, and fear as our kids thirst for independence. It is a time of experimentation, of sorting out for themselves their standards, their choices for life. The world offers enticements—alcohol, drugs, sex, and even though we have tried to root them in the Word, we can't be sure our children will make the right choices, the Christian choices.

Dr. McCormick feels that although many children receive Christ in their early years, true cognitive development, when a child can really understand spiritual concepts, doesn't come till the teens. This, she believes, is the critical time. Many of us recognize this, and it adds to our fear. At the time when our children are busy pulling away from us, we want to have the most impact.

Dr. McCormick goes on to say that whether or not a child incorporates a mother's values during these years depends on the sort of mother she is. "If she is a controlling, pushy person, the child will pull away. And this is so difficult, because the mother wants so much for her child to know the Lord."

The most important guideline to encourage your teen's spirituality, according to Dr. McCormick? "Let go."

That's scary for Christian parents. But remember, "letting go" doesn't mean that you stop praying for your children, that you have no rules or that you can never say a thing. It does mean that you treat your child with the respect you give other adults, allowing him more and more freedom to make his own decisions—and his own mistakes.

For Pat, the byword during these years was "little by little." Long lectures were out, but her teens would accept a little wisdom here, a tidbit of advice there.

## OUR ADULT CHILDREN

The good news is that if your children do not know the Lord by their teen years, all is not lost. Many of us received the Lord as adults, some of us after our children were grown, and we may mourn what we did not—could not—give to them spiritually. "If only I'd known the Lord then" is our cry.

Rather than lament what might have been, trust in God's timing and know that your adult children, like you, may also be late bloomers.

Of course, you cannot, nor should you try to, coerce them into coming to the Lord. But often if you use wisdom and restraint and continue to listen and be available your grown children can become your friends. Rich discussions of the meaning and purpose of life may unfold, giving you opportunities to share what your faith means to you. And be assured, they are watching you. Be open about your traumas as well as your triumphs so that the witness of your life and your prayers will continue to impact their lives.

## HOW TO ENRICH THE SHARING OF YOUR FAITH

*Pray with your children.* Pray aloud with your children—even from infancy. Plan regular times of prayer, such as when you tuck them into bed, before meals, or as they leave for school or play. When they begin to talk, encourage them to join in.

Pray with your children on the spur of the moment, too, about the nitty-gritties of life. Pray that a skinned knee will stop hurting, that they will pass a test, or for whatever else is important to them.

Memorized prayers are good, but also encourage your children to talk to God spontaneously about their concerns. Sally, noticing that her children's praying had become mechanical, decided to model meaningful prayers for them by taking a turn during their bedtime prayers. "It was incredibly difficult," she remembers, "to pray open, honest prayers that would make sense to a four- and six-year-old."

She struggled each night to be real, yet to share only what

was appropriate for her small children. But it was worth the effort, as gradually her children's prayers became more genuine.

One adult now reminisces, "It was so important to me that my mother prayed with me, rather than just listening while I prayed. She, too, humbled herself before God."

Let your children ask God for what they want. Trust that the Lord is able to teach them to accept his no as well as his yes. Pat worried that if God didn't answer some of her children's prayers, they might lose their faith in him. The children's requests sometimes seemed so impossible. But looking back, God's track record was amazing.

If your husband feels antagonistic about prayer, you may have to limit it to times when you are alone with the children. However, some unbelieving husbands don't object to certain kinds of prayer, so don't be afraid to ask.

When Sally suggested saying grace before dinner "to teach the kids not to take everything for granted," her husband was happy to let each of the children take turns asking the blessing. And Marcy's husband doesn't object to grace at family gatherings.

*Listen to them.* Availability is the key word here. Really listening to our children communicates to them that they are important, worthwhile, loved just as they are. And if you don't listen to your child, he will learn in a hurry not to listen to you.

Many of us have regular special times of close communication with our children, such as before bedtime or naptime, or over snacks when they come home from school, thus establishing a habit of open lines of communication.

But often the best exchanges are completely unscheduled, quite unexpectedly initiated by our offspring. Indeed, their timing may leave a lot to be desired. But when they want to talk, we need to be ready to listen.

Bev, who had stepped outside to pick up the evening paper, found herself caught up in a discussion on sexual promiscuity with her teenage son while standing in the middle of the driveway. This moment might never come again in quite the same way, so she stopped and listened and answered his questions as honestly and scripturally as she could.

We have all had similar experiences with younger children, as with the five-year-old who asks, "Where did I come from?" when you are preparing Christmas dinner for twenty; the eight-year-old who wonders, "Who made God?" when you are struggling with a stopped-up sink.

Sometimes, however, you will sense that something is bothering a child, and you may want to arrange a time when he might feel comfortable sharing. Driving together in the car or walking together is sometimes more freeing to a child than sitting eyeball-to-eyeball with you. Or you may want to make an ice cream or lunch date.

Even your children's illnesses may prove times of openness when deep feelings and spiritual truths could be plumbed. Some times you will find you can be the one to introduce certain topics. Other times, they will be prompted by the child. "When did you get to be your own person?" was one leading question fed to Bev by a flu-stricken son.

Who knows? If you encourage open exchanges, you might even be the one to lead your child to the Lord. Betty J. M. Bube, in *What They Did Right,*[2] tells how at age nine or ten, she confided her fear of death to her mother. Her mother's sympathetic, scriptural response prompted the daughter to ask, "Mother, am I saved? I really want to be."

And it was then, she wrote, "My mother had the joy of leading me to the Lord Jesus Christ."

*Share with them what God is doing in your life.* It is so important not to just teach them about God but to share some of your personal spiritual life with them. Your child needs to hear how God answers your prayers, and how he meets specific personal and financial needs, how he is using you in other people's lives. Don't be afraid to describe what he is teaching you in your own life or even to ask, "Can you see how God is working in this situation?"

Again, this isn't easy for most of us. You will need God's help in sorting out what and how to share, but your children need to see your Christianity in true life situations.

*Read to your children.* Never underestimate the power of reading the Bible, Christian books, and other favorites to your children. You can begin very early with simple, colorfully illustrated Bible stories, then move along to books that keep pace with your children's development. It is a wonderful way to instill a love of the Word and a love of reading in your child.

Build a library for your children, and don't neglect taking them to the Christian and secular book stores and the library to make their own selections. ("Boy, Dave, you missed the best time!" exclaimed six-year-old Bryan to his older brother as he burst into the house, arms loaded with library books.)

Seek exciting, well-put-together stories. Who wants to plod through dull content or a poor ending? Look for stories where wrong is ultimately wrong and right is right. The quality of Christian fiction is improving. And don't ignore the classics you grew up reading. Many secular children's books also make strong moral points.

Reading together brings such special times of closeness. It may be the longest period of time a child will sit on your lap, or snuggle against you. And reading aloud, you have the chance to emphasize a special point that could otherwise be overlooked, or to ask and answer questions, or discuss a moot idea.

So don't stop when your children are able to read to themselves. Stretch it out just as long as you possibly can—even if read-aloud-time diminishes to vacations away from home. (Bev and her mother continued to read aloud to each other during summer vacations when she was in college!)

If you have trouble choosing good books for your children, *A Parent's Guide to Christian Books for Children*[3] might be a very helpful booklet.

*Sing a joyful song.* It is scriptural and it is such a delight to sing our praises to the Lord! Further, biblical choruses provide a marvelous way for children to learn Scripture. Many adults say their fondest memories are of their mothers singing together with them in the car, the kitchen, the bathroom, or out walking together.

And in *What They Did Right,* Beatrice Cairns remembers how her mother "lay beside me in the dark, singing me to sleep, and the sweetness of her voice on the chorus of a favorite hymn, 'How marvelous, how wonderful, is my Savior's love for me.'"[4] What a wonderful, warm way to allay a child's fear of the dark, to make him feel secure in God's love.

Even if you weren't gifted with the voice of an angel—even if you can't carry a tune, your very young children won't know the difference. And you will find excellent Christian records and tapes to help you. It is fun to "sing along."

*Special Projects.* Many mothers have created their own projects or even games to help their children understand basic precepts, as well as the meaning of specific holidays.

In the *Guideposts'* 1982 Christmas card[5] Lynne Laukhuf told how her family put Christ into their Christmas. They decided to prepare the bed for the baby Jesus in their manger scene. Each time they did a kindness for someone else, they would place a piece of straw in the empty crib. As small deeds were performed—from sending hand-drawn pictures to grandparents to emptying the dishwasher—the crib began to fill. Thus the family prepared itself for his coming "in the best way of all ways—by giving ourselves to him in little gifts of love."

A variation on this is a family that draws names each week. The goal: during the following week to do a kindness for that person without anyone knowing who did it.

Other families make a family table centerpiece of an advent wreath, with four candles, one to be lit each week in advent, while the family sings "O Come, O Come, Emmanuel."

Do simple projects with a time limit. Many are fun and exciting at first but become drudgery when they drag on and on. If your family likes games, try some of the Bible trivia, Bible memory, or Christian board games for children. Christian records and videocassettes can also enrich your children's lives.

## WHAT ABOUT CHURCH?

By your own regular attendance at *Sunday services* you make a clear statement to your children of the central role of the church in your life—for worship, study, and fellowship. If your attitude is, "This is what we do on Sunday morning; there's nowhere else I'd want to be," you tend to pass on your enthusiasm.

Of course, your ability to attend church regularly depends to some extent on your husband's attitude. A barely believing husband probably won't object and may go with you, at least some of the time. But an unbelieving husband may feel you are cheating him of his weekend or his time with you and the kids. Then you will need to find compromises.

Perhaps he would be happy with a weekend a month when you can plan activities as a family. Or maybe you and the children can become involved Sunday evening or in weekday activities that can, to some extent, take the place of Sunday morning church. Ask God to help you be creative in finding time to worship, fellowship, and receive teaching for you and your children.

*Sunday school and youth activities.* "A strong Sunday school program has been so important to us," declared Jeanne, whose children are committed Christians, though her husband is still not a believer. "I started them in Sunday school at about two," she recalled, "and as they grew, they became involved in choir and other youth activities. My daughter has gone out on a mission to a rural area for two summers now. It seems to me that if you get one started in this pattern, the next one tends to follow along. My husband never objected. In fact, he liked the 'strong moral teaching' they received."

Since most teachers and youth workers are volunteers, the quality of leadership varies greatly from church to church, from class to class, and from activity to activity. We think it is especially important that the children of unbelieving fathers *like* going to church. We need to look for programs where our children will be exposed to mature Christians and receive biblical teaching presented in an enjoyable way.

If your husband doesn't object, you may want to get involved so you can see firsthand what your children are experiencing.

Consistency in attendance is important. If the men and women who dedicate their time to teaching Sunday school are to affect your children's lives, they need to have the opportunity to build, week after week, to help them to grow a little bit at a time.

A bonus of Sunday school and church activities is your children's exposure to men in leadership and to Christ-centered families where they see, firsthand, that it is not unmanly or wimpy for a man to commit his life to the Lord.

*Church camps.* In the summertime, by all means consider the vacation Bible schools and day camps offered by many churches. Many adults have fond memories of such activities as sculpting Bible mottos, including "Love one another," in the sand at the beach, hikes up a nearby canyon, hot dog cookouts, as well as praying and singing God's praises together.

Remember, too, a week or two at Christian camp can be a life-changing experience for a youngster. One mother described how all three of her children received the Lord at Forest Home summer camp in the mountains of southern California. "That was the mountaintop experience," she noted.

For young people in the middle grades and high school,

many churches offer more adventurous activities, such as ski weekends, river trips, project weekends to the inner city, or a work camp to a mission station or church in a foreign country. These experiences can bring spiritual breakthroughs, encourage teens to re-think their futures, to look beyond themselves and establish Christian friendships both with peers and adults.

## BUT WHAT DOES DAD BELIEVE?

Inevitably, questions arise about the difference in your beliefs and your husband's. It is vital that you not put down your husband, or tell your child that Dad's wrong, bad, or a "miserable sinner." (So are you!) This, in fact, is your golden opportunity to model unconditional love, as you honestly admit your differences while assuring the child how much you love Daddy, accepting him just the way he is. Try to stress his good qualities. And do encourage your child to pray with you for Dad to know the Lord.

## WHEN DAD SAYS, "NONE OF THAT GOD STUFF FOR MY KIDS!"

Marilyn talked frequently with her three-year-old about Jesus and his love. Then one evening her unbelieving husband asked his son, "Bobby, who loves you?" and waited expectantly for Bobby to respond, "Daddy!"

Instead, he replied, "Je-sus!" The scene that followed was not a pretty thing, and it culminated with the father roaring, "Don't you dare fill my son's head with this nonsense about Jesus!"

What are you to do if you are in a situation like Marilyn's? You want so much to share Jesus with your child. But do you dare? Truly, our hearts go out to you. And we urge you to remember, God has promised never to try us beyond what we are able to bear and has said he will show us a way out (1 Cor. 10:13).

Peter and John also found themselves in hot water because of sharing the Lord. When the Sanhedrin commanded them to stop speaking about Jesus, they replied, "Judge for yourselves whether it is right in God's sight to obey you rather than God. For we cannot help speaking about what we have seen and heard" (Acts 4:19-20).

As you consider this Scripture and how it may apply to you, you may want to stop for a time to fast and pray. Go over again the principles for dealing with differences in values mentioned in an earlier chapter. We believe that God has a way for you to walk through this.

It may help to assure your husband that the Bible teaches children good values, such as honesty, caring about others, and loving and obeying their fathers. Some wives have found that when they take a firm stand, their husbands gradually relent.

In those cases where a father makes life truly unpleasant for you or your child, a growing faith can be a rock and "high tower," a real comfort in time of trouble.

## THE BOTTOM LINE IS . . .

Just as we saw earlier that we cannot give faith to our husbands, we must recognize that we cannot give it to our children. It is a gift of the Lord.

The writer of Proverbs urged us to "train a child in the way he should go, and when he is old he will not turn from it" (22:6). And Paul promised the Corinthians "For the unbelieving husband has been sanctified through his wife, and the unbelieving wife has been sanctified through her believing husband. Otherwise your children would be unclean, but as it is, they are holy" (1 Cor. 7:14). That means our children are set apart unto God in a special way. What a promise!

Although we can't point to an official survey, we are encouraged by the wives with unbelieving or foot-dragging Christian husbands whom we interviewed. For the majority of those who raised their children with Christian values and instruction told us their children have committed their lives to the Lord.

A not infrequent pattern is that the child may follow the mother's lead until the teen years. At this point, there may be a turning away, followed often by a return and commitment or recommitment.

Since none of us is perfect, we will not be perfect mothers. We will blow it. We will lose our temper with our children at times when we should remain calm. We will be too rushed sometimes to listen carefully to them. We will too often find we don't have the right words to share about the Lord or enough wisdom to help when their need is great.

But God still loves us and our children. And His love is enough to cover all our failures. Through Joel, God promised Israel, after he had destroyed their crops in judgment, that he would make up to them "for the years that the locusts have eaten" (2:25). Surely he also loves our children enough to restore to them all they have missed by our coming to Christ late and by having an unbelieving father. We claim that for our children and yours!

## QUESTIONS FOR FURTHER STUDY AND GROUP DISCUSSION

1. Most of us have days when we wonder why we ever wanted children. What does the Bible say about the value and the difficulty of having children?

> *Genesis 1:28*
> *Genesis 3:16*
> *Psalm 127:3-5*
> *Psalm 128:1-6*
> *1 Timothy 2:13-15*

2. What scriptural promises can we hang on to as we bring up our children with an unbelieving or barely believing father? Here are some to start you thinking. Add your own favorites.

*Proverbs 3:5-8*
*Isaiah 40:29-31*
*Isaiah 49:25*
*Isaiah 54:11-13*
*Acts 16:27-33, especially verse 31*
*1 Corinthians 7:14*

3. If one or both your parents were Christians, what part of your faith did you "catch" from them?

4. If our children "catch" our Christianity by living with us, what do you want your children to assimilate from your life? Are there still aspects of your life you do not want them to copy? Ask the Holy Spirit to help you identify these and seek his help in changing.

5. Look up the following verses to better understand God's unconditional love for us.

*John 3:16-17*
*Romans 5:6-8*
*Philippians 2:3-8*
*1 John 4:16-19*

Now reread the section "Love Your Children" in this chapter. In your own words, define unconditional love. Define approval. Give a personal example of unconditional love in your family and an example of approval.

6. Scripture directs us to train our children in godly ways, but it also reminds us not to provoke them to anger (Eph. 6:4). If possible, we want to avoid causing anger or rebellion against God in our children, knowing it might be encouraged by their unbelieving dads. What methods do you use to train your children? Which cause the most anger in them? Which produce the least anger?

7. Now see if you can identify some of the characteristics of

a godly mother. In the following passages, who is the mother? What does Scripture tell us directly or indirectly about her character or the ways she raised her children?

> *Exodus 2:1-15*
> *Numbers 12:3*
> *Hebrews 11:23-28*
>
> *1 Samuel 1-2:11, 18-21, 3:19, 7:15*
>
> *Proverbs 31:10-31*
>
> *Luke 1:26-56, 2:18-19, 41-52*
> *John 19:26-27*
> *Acts 1:14*
>
> *Acts 16:1-3*
> *1 Timothy 1:1-2★*
> *2 Timothy 1:1-5★*

★(Timothy's father was either no longer living or was possibly an unbelieving father.)

8. What do you do to share the Lord with your children? What is most difficult for you about the sharing? What new ideas did you get from this chapter?

9. Does your husband object to your telling or teaching your children about Christ? If so, how do you handle this? Pray especially for anyone in your group whose husband is antagonistic about such sharing.

**Pray together for your husbands to grow in their ability to be good fathers and that your children will come to know the Lord and grow into mature Christians.**

# TEN
# YOU CAN STILL HAVE A MINISTRY

Gail felt honored when the nominating committee approached her to become vice president of a Christian club for women. She knew she could do the job. But her heart sank as she remembered that the club held two retreats a year, several all-day Saturday seminars, and a Christian banquet—all of which she would be expected to attend. Gail knew her husband, an unbeliever, would "have a fit" over her being away from him so much.

Samantha loved children and brimmed with ideas on how to make learning about God fun for them. So she was excited to be asked to teach Sunday school. But the Sunday school teachers' meeting was a potluck dinner on the first Saturday of each month. She was sure her husband would resent her leaving him at home to feed the kids on a Saturday night.

From the first day Ann began studying the Bible with the women in her church, she wanted to be a teacher. Finally, she was asked to lead a new class. But she wasn't sure she was fully qualified. After all, her husband wasn't a believer. Maybe she wasn't a "good enough" Christian to teach.

We want to serve our Lord, to share with others what he has done for us, but sometimes Christian service can be such a hassle for those of us married to unbelieving husbands.

Perhaps we should just let others handle these ministries. Surely God would understand.

## BUT WE ARE ALL CALLED TO MINISTER

The Apostle Paul wrote, "We are God's workmanship, created in Christ Jesus to do good works, which God prepared in advance for us to do" (Eph. 2:10).

And Peter reminded us, "God has given each of you some special abilities; be sure to use them to help each other, passing on to others God's many kinds of blessings" (1 Pet. 4:10, TLB).

Some of us are natural teachers, like Cathy, who always thinks in terms of organizing, clarifying, and illustrating to make her material memorable. Others seem to be born with an unusual flair for hospitality, like Gail, who entertains easily and with a warmth and graciousness that makes everyone in her home feel welcome and at ease. Still others have the aptitude for administration, or for sharing the gospel, or encouraging, or serving, or giving to others.

As we grow in the Lord and in our love of him, most of us yearn to serve him and to bless others by using as fully as possible whatever gifts he has given us. But as the wives of unbelieving or barely believing husbands, we tend to run into two problems: the dilemma of how to serve effectively while still honoring our husbands and a sense that we're not fully qualified to minister.

## YOUR HUSBAND AND YOUR MINISTRY

Many of us feel we are held back in our ministry for the Lord by our husbands. "Oh, if I could just be free, I could do so much more for the Lord," we cry. "If my husband wasn't so jealous of my time." "If he'd just come to the Lord!" "If he'd expect a little less of me at home!"

In our eagerness to serve the Lord it is easy to become impatient, frustrated. Consider some of the areas of friction, and perhaps we can find some solutions.

*Your ministry may separate you—occasionally or often.* Does your Christian involvement take place during the hours your husband is at work, or busy with his own activities? If so it probably causes little or no friction, assuming, of course, that you still have time to fulfill your responsibilities as a wife.

But sometimes evening meetings may bring you home late, after he is in bed, and cause you to drag the next morning. And how often do you leave your husband and children home, choosing to minister to others?

Then there is the time you and your husband are at home together. Do you spend hours on the phone, planning church functions or perhaps counseling or praying with other believers? And if fellow Christians drop by for fellowship or counseling, does your unbelieving or uninterested husband have to retreat to another room of the house?

*Your ministry may offend your husband.* If your husband is a truly dedicated atheist, agnostic, or has another belief system, he may feel belligerent, defensive—even embarrassed by your involvement in Christian leadership. Women in highly visible ministries may especially find this irritates their husbands.

*"You work hard and you don't even get paid!"* "My husband is completely unable to understand how anybody can devote so much time to an endeavor without being paid," declares Belinda, who teaches Bible stories to Good News clubs of neighborhood children. "We don't need extra money; it's the principle. He thinks what I do is a waste of time."

As Christians we love to see people helped and know God will reward us in eternity. But to our husbands, that is foolishness.

*"Why does she do all that?"* It is so difficult for most husbands to understand why we want to spend our time in ministry. We know it is because the Lord told us to, and we

want to glorify him, right?

Of course that is our main focus. But we are human and for most of us, other motivations often slip in, sometimes without our realizing it.

One motivation is our need for approval. We have talked in earlier chapters about the difference between love and approval, but many of us, in seeking our husbands' expression of love, look for it in the form of approval. Or as Anne put it, "If just once he'd tell me that the house looks nice when I've spent the whole day cleaning. Or if occasionally he'd say dinner is good. Or that I'm doing an OK job with the kids."

Men don't seem to easily or naturally verbalize their approval, so, hungering for it, many of us reach outside the home. It seems to us that the ranks of volunteerism are filled with women seeking approval they don't receive at home.

In the secular world it feels good to be praised as president of the PTA or room mother or Campfire leader or hospital fund drive chairman. And in the Christian realm it is satisfying to be lauded for your skill at handling registration for the women's retreat or being in charge of the spring luncheon or teaching Bible study.

We feel it's normal and natural and OK for you to enjoy those strokes, as long as you understand what is happening and don't let it get out of hand. But do be careful that you are not like the people Paul referred to who serve "their own appetites" rather than the Lord (Rom. 16:18).

Another motivation for ministry is our need for results. We may reach out in frustration, when our efforts on the home front seem to no avail or when our husbands don't seem to progress at all in their relationship with the Lord. The grass of service can look a lot greener outside our own yard. Or as Greta expressed it, "I might as well try someplace where I can do some good. My chances would be a lot better on skid row or in darkest Africa than in my own home."

Again, it is normal to want to see results for your efforts and it can be so gratifying when, in your ministry to others, you are privileged to see lives change as people respond to the Lord. But what message does your husband receive from your commitment?

*"She prefers church—or God—to me."* When a wife is so busily involved in her ministry, a husband may begin to feel he is no longer important. Unfortunately, he may be quite accurate in his assessment that she prefers the things of the Lord to him.

The trap is that as we become more and more involved, we begin to feel an acute sense of responsibility to our ministry. After all, think of all those people in the body who are depending on us. They need us! We must be trustworthy, faithful, reliable! Sometimes we lose touch with our priorities. We need, then, to review them.

Who is first to us? Remember, our intimate, personal relationship with the Lord comes first, above all else. And next? Our husbands. No, not our responsibility to others, God-given though it may seem to us. Our husbands, and our families, come before the church and our Christian friends. So be very, very careful to distinguish between the things of the Lord, and the Lord.

But, you may cry, that means that my ministry is diminished. No, it does not. This is what Carmen discovered. Living in Guatamala, she began with a small teaching ministry, which gradually required more and more time. Then came the squeeze play of trying to fulfill her main priority—her responsibilities at home—first, and also to maintain her ministry. "How can I find time to be the housewife and mother my husband wants me to be and also to be the servant the Lord wants me to be?" she wondered.

Then God put "complete brakes" on her ministry by showing her she was illuminating other people without setting an example in her home. "It was as though God said, 'No, you're going to serve and practice everything you learned—but at home now. You be there as a servant of the living God.' He showed me a different dimension of his ministry."

Or, as another wife pointed out, "My husband is my first ministry, though he doesn't know it."

When our priorities are straight at home we have a firm foundation from which to move out to the world. Carmen learned she could be content and fulfilled at home. Later, she and her American husband moved with their family to the United States. "I came in obedience, but I thought for sure that was the end of any ministry outside my home."

She was astonished when God gave her a whole new mission field, teaching Hispanic women in California. However, now she testifies, "My priorities today follow his wisdom, not mine."

## THE KEY TO PEACE AT HOME

Without exception, the women we interviewed who successfully balance their marriage and their ministry begin by consulting their husbands first.

"I go to him and I ask him what he thinks about any given project," Linda told us. "I outline, as honestly as I can, what the time demands are likely to be. And I also share my heart—how important the job is to me."

She added, "There is almost no conflict if I truly put my husband first, and I tell him from the beginning that this is my desire. Because his work schedule varies, he's sometimes home on weekdays. And if he wants to do something then and I have a class to teach at the same time, I go with him. Of course, I always have a backup waiting in the wings to take over the class. And, actually, it doesn't happen too often. But it's important that he knows I am willing and that he does come first."

Polly takes a similar but firmer approach. "I try, for every commitment in ministry, to ask my husband's permission first, knowing that later on trials will come. This way, I have his word, and I can say to him, 'I have this commitment and I cannot just leave the class right now. I took it on because you've given me permission.'"

Polly told us she has found not only that the Lord always honors obedience, but that she honors God more by obeying him than by pushing forward with her teaching against her husband's will. Moreover, "When my will is in God's perfect will, I've actually seen him change my husband's heart," she declared. "He will say to me, 'You go on. I know this is something that makes you happy. You go ahead.'"

Do you ask him about absolutely everything? Inquiring about each tiny detail may, in some men, trigger automatic "no's." Other men don't want to be bothered. We generally discuss only things that will affect them.


## BUT ARE YOU WORTHY TO MINISTER?

Do you ever wonder if you really should minister? After all, you don't have an on-fire-for-the-Lord husband. Maybe someone else could be a better example or do a better job.

We all have times of self-doubt, times when we are crushingly aware of our shortcomings. Yet God isn't looking for perfect people, but for those who know they have been saved by a great God. Our ministry may be most effective when we know we are not worthy, and therefore must totally depend on God's love, his mercy and grace.

*But others hint that we should not minister.* Occasionally, in a few churches and Christian organizations, we sense a subtle but unmistakable implication that because our husbands are not all-out believers, we are not quite whole persons for the Lord. People are usually very "nice" about it, very gentle, but the message is clear: we don't fully qualify to serve.

Kerry, an experienced teacher, had done extensive research on marriage and husband-wife relationships. But when the marriage classes were set up at her church, the woman in charge made it clear that she wanted only teachers with "ideal" Christian marriages. Kerry knew she was automatically disqualified because her husband wasn't involved in the church.

It seemed never to occur to this woman that because Kerry had struggled through many difficulties in her marriage, she may have been far more qualified. She could help others confront the hard places better than a woman with a "perfect" marriage who never had to deal with problems and who might have no idea why her marriage was so wonderful.

Fortunately, God opened the door for Kerry to teach elsewhere, and lives were changed through her compassion and understanding. "It was a relief," she admits, "to find that God didn't consider me a second-class citizen!"

In another church, a woman with an unbelieving husband, when nominated for the women's ministry board, was almost passed by. The explanation was given that she didn't fit the requirements for a key leader because she didn't always attend church potlucks and picnics. Never mind that she wasn't there because she chose instead to be with her husband. Fortunately, the church leadership ultimately was wise enough to understand and accept her great capacity for ministering to the body.

Still another woman was told by "well-meaning" relatives that because of her unbelieving husband God could not bless her, much less use her in ministry!

*Wives of unbelievers are not disqualified.* Nowhere in the Bible can we find a passage stating that a woman should be disqualified, either from a full relationship with the Lord or from ministry for the Lord, because her husband is not a pillar of the church. In fact, as we discussed in an earlier chapter, every believer is a priest. We have been gathered into his kingdom and made priests of God the Father (Rev. 1:6).

Our relationship is one-on-one with God the Father and

God the Son. We don't need a third party—our husband or anyone else—to qualify us before God. As one woman pointed out, we each have an individual walk with the Lord; it is not a couple's walk.

So if you feel called to minister, seek the Lord until you find your special niche. Ministry, of course, doesn't mean only speaking to conferences or serving as president of the women's organization. It is the use of any of the gifts, which are vitally important for the whole of the body of Christ.

But a word of caution is in order. If there has been some hesitation among your church leadership over your ministry, you may be tempted to go it alone, just you and God. We would remind you that this isn't scriptural. As wives of unbelievers we especially need to have a church family. Seek fellowship within the body of Christ that will provide you with a home base from which you can go out. Find people in your church to give you guidance and encouragement—people with the wisdom to help keep your ministry or service in good scriptural balance.

## TRUST GOD TO PROVIDE
## JUST THE RIGHT MINISTRY FOR YOU

One wise leader advised us to "watch out not to make a priority of serving your ministry instead of serving the Lord. Your trust and walk of faith is by obedience to him and to your husband. God will provide areas of service and sisters to help you."

Again and again, we have watched God provide perfect ministries to women who walk in obedience with him.

*Often it can be accomplished during the day.* Many husbands have no objections to activities that take their wives away occasionally, but others react negatively to time apart. If you are wise about planning your scheduling of time, you may be able to prepare lessons and teach Bible studies, visit the ill, take dinners to others, hostess coffees and luncheons—all during the time your husband is at work or busy with other activities. Be a good steward of that time and balance your service and your attention to the home.

Agnes invites the elderly women of her church to luncheon once a month. Her family considers this a dividend for them, because there is always a special dish or dessert remaining for their dinner. Joan, who lives in a neighborhood with many widows, makes soup for them one day of the week, and her kids call it "souper Wednesday," because they also enjoy the homemade minestrone, chicken with fresh vegetables, or other hearty soup that evening.

*It has elements approved by the husbands.* At this very moment, our husbands are pleased that we will soon have a book in print. And Jan's husband, who has little time available to serve the needy, is proud that she takes food and clothing from the church each week to a nearby mission. Nancy's husband, who recognizes her singing ability, is happy when she is asked to sing in church and usually comes to listen and support her.

And though your husband may not realize it, he may benefit from the fruits of your ministry, as you grow in wisdom, sensitivity, and skills. As food chairman of a women's luncheon Sandy learned to plan food for a large crowd, so when her husband needed to entertain fifty business associates she could tell him, "That's no problem for me."

*Some husbands may even help.* "I was scared at first to ask, but I really needed help in organizing a list of the various areas of talent within our body," one lady told us. "I finally asked my husband if his computer could do it. He seemed glad I brought it to him, and came up with a great printout that saved me hours of time."

Pat's husband has made photocopies of her Bible study lessons for years. And when Bev found herself in a sticky situation in her writing ministry, her husband gave wise, unbiased counsel.

You may be surprised at your husband's willingness to

help or to give advice. Why not ask?

*It may make use of your experience.* Marty admits she is a compulsive eater. Who, then, better understands the problems of women in a weight reduction program? She volunteered her time one day to fill in for another worker and became so popular with the clients that she now serves regularly.

After years as an executive secretary, Gwen retired. But she gives two days a week to work in the church office, where her expertise is invaluable.

Myrna grew up in a home where there was plenty of southern hospitality and it seemed natural to open her home to missionaries and church groups. But she says, "I always ask my husband first. Although he isn't a Christian, it pleases him that his family enjoys sharing their home. He even helps prepare and clean up afterwards because he understands it's a lot of work to entertain."

Carol was devastated when she discovered her son had been molested by a male neighbor. As she gradually put the pieces of their lives back together, she hungered to help other children resist or get help after such a traumatic experience. When she discovered a nearby police department training people to go into elementary school classrooms to talk about molestation, she signed up. She has since alerted friends that the "nice man" who took so many pictures of their son was a producer of kiddie porn pictures. Moreover, she helped identify a number of abused children in her local schools.

And look what we are doing! We are using the experience we have gained in our years as wives of unbelieving husbands to write this book.

*Don't forget to minister to your family, too.* Of course we are all called to minister within our families, but sometimes, like our Guatemalan friend Carmen, we push that calling away. It isn't as glamorous or rewarding as being an officer of your women's group at church or speaking at women's luncheons.

The variety of service our families need is endless. Many women with small children find that for a season, their ministry is their immediate family. What could be more important than teaching our children God's love, to provide a secure base for self-esteem? Explaining to a child where God lives or praying for "ow-ies" may not appear to have worldwide impact, but who knows what God's call on your children may be?

Our extended family may also have pressing needs. Kim traveled halfway across the country to help her sister after her surgery. And Tammy is concerned about her niece, a new believer who lives three thousand miles away. So Tammy disciples her by telephone once a week during the low-rate calling hours.

Then, as our children grow up, our parents begin to need us more. Leanne takes her mother-in-law shopping once a week and Cindy tries to have her mother over for dinner often since her father died. Toni finds that her father wants to talk about God more and more as he grows older.

And let's hear it for the grandchildren! While Renee's daughter works three days a week, Renee takes care of her grandaughter. What a pleasure it is for this grandmother to begin telling a new generation about Jesus.

## YOUR MINISTRY WILL BE PERFECTLY SUITED TO YOU

God wants to give us the desires of our hearts, and in his time he will provide us with exactly the right ministry. Alice wasn't at all sure why she took extensive training in the effective use of color, line, and style in clothing. Today she is giving the handicapped a huge confidence boost by teaching them how to look their very best.

Jane had never made a speech in her life, but for years, she suffered from bulimia (binge eating followed by purging her body of the food). When, through Christian counseling, she overcame this eating disorder, she found herself in great demand as a speaker for groups ranging from high school girls to professional business women.

If you feel frustrated in your attempts at ministry, don't despair. Judy told us she had learned when doors closed to her to see the Lord, not her husband, as the closer. "Usually it's worked out for the best," she said.

Our experience is that God will show you the right times and places to serve if you ask him, if you are patient in seeking his answer. Sometimes when your efforts seem blocked it's simply God saying, "Not yet."

Remember, too, ministry is not static, so don't become boxed into what you perceive as "my ministry." Most of us will serve in a number of capacities and they will change as we grow and as the circumstances of our lives vary. So don't limit God. You may think you have only one talent, but perhaps he is urging you to try something new.

Pat felt comfortable as a Bible teacher, but she never dreamed God wanted her to write. Since she didn't write well, she thought God was making a mistake or she wasn't hearing him correctly when he began to press her to try writing. It took a lot of learning. But if she had refused to be obedient years ago, she would have missed the opportunity to participate in writing this book.

Bev always knew she wasn't cut out to be a teacher. Her knees shook at the very idea, and she was sure she would faint dead away if she tried to speak to a group of three or more. But one day she prayed, "Lord, don't let me lock myself into writing as my ministry if there's something else you want me to do." After she coauthored *Change for the Better,* she was asked to conduct seminars on menopause and, yes, her knees shook but, no, she didn't faint dead away. This gave her the courage to say yes to teaching Bible studies in her mother-in-law's retirement home.

It is so exciting to see where the Lord will take us—what vessels we can be in his service if we listen to him!

So be open to his leading. Believe with us that, "No eye

has seen, no ear has heard, no mind has conceived what God has prepared for those who love him" (1 Cor. 2:9).

## QUESTIONS FOR FURTHER STUDY AND GROUP DISCUSSION

1. Some have questioned whether a woman should ever be in leadership or have a ministry. What is the woman's ministry described in the following Scriptures?

> *Exodus 15:20-21*
> *Judges 4:1-9*
> *Luke 2:36-38*
> *Luke 8:1-3*
> *Acts 9:36-42*
> *Acts 21:8-9*
> *Titus 2:3-5*

2. List the variety of ministries, services, and gifts we see in Scripture.

> *Romans 12:4-15*
> *1 Corinthians 12*
> *Ephesians 4:4-16*

Have you ministered or served in any of these areas? Do you have any dreams, any burdens for ministry?

3. Do you think your husband or people in the church will hold you back from what God has really called you to do? Consider the following Scriptures before you answer.

> *Psalm 37:4*
> *Proverbs 18:16*
> *Romans 8:28-39*

Share a time when you felt held back because of your unbelieving or barely believing husband. Share a time when God surprised you and opened the door for ministry.

4. Reread the section "Your Husband and Your Ministry" in this chapter. Have you experienced any of these conflicts between your ministry and your marriage? Have you tried any of the suggestions in the chapter? Were they helpful? Do you have any other ideas that might help others? Share an area of friction—something, however, that will not embarrass your husband.

5. In what ways has God used your past experience in service for him?

6. Is there anything about your ministry that pleases your husband?

7. Many times we are unaware that we have helped others and we become discouraged. Thank those members of your group who have specifically ministered to you. Identify any areas or gifts the Lord has used so that you can encourage these women in their ministries.

**Pray that God will guide each of you into service for him and that he will help you see how it will bless your husband.**

# ELEVEN
# YOU CAN BE CONTENT!

A minister listened patiently as we told him we were writing a book about how to be the contented wife of an unbelieving husband. He shook his head and laughed. "There isn't any such thing," he declared.

Oh, how we disagree! Perhaps he hasn't found any contented wives among the women who come to him for counseling. But we have talked with them, taught them in a summer Bible study-workshop. And we ourselves have experienced a new depth of contentment in the process of writing this book.

Yes, we thought we were content when we began, but as we researched and studied the Word and tossed ideas back and forth, we found that there is much more! And we are convinced that, yes, you *can* be content.

## WHAT DO WE MEAN BY "CONTENT"?
Let us define our terms. We looked first at Webster's unabridged dictionary and learned that our English word stems from the Latin *contentus,* which can be broken down into *con,* meaning together, and the verb *tenere,* to hold in, or to contain. Content, then, literally means "held; contained within limits; hence, quiet; not disturbed; having a mind at

peace, easy; satisfied." Contentment is a resting or satisfaction of the mind, without disquiet.

We are convinced that every believing woman, no matter what her husband's spiritual status, can experience that sense of rest in the Lord because she knows the supreme source of rest, Jesus. Remember how he told us, "Come to me . . . and I will give you rest"? (Matt. 11:28). And every woman of faith can also know the "satisfaction of mind" that focuses on the Lord, rather than on the situation, trusting his stated purpose to work all things together for good (Rom. 8:28).

Contentment is quite a different thing from happiness, which Webster defines as "the agreeable sensation that springs from the enjoyment of good; that state of a being in which his desires are gratified by the enjoyment of pleasure without pain."

To be happy is to be lucky, fortunate, successful. ("I'm so happy you're here." "I'm happy with the way this program worked out.") Obviously, it depends on the circumstances and the absence of pain. Contentment does not.

We found more insight into the word *content* in *Vine's Expository Dictionary of Old and New Testament Words.* The Greek word *autarkes* may be translated "sufficient in oneself" (*autos,* self; *arkeo,* sufficient or "self sufficient, adequate, needing no assistance).["1]

How can we be sufficient in ourselves? Only through Christ within us. When we draw upon him, the difficulties in our lives needn't defeat us. Our moods, our thoughts, our emotions needn't vacillate from good to bad to terrible, according to our circumstances. This must have been what Paul meant when he said, "I have learned to be content whatever the circumstances" (Phil. 4:11), or as the King James Version puts it, "in whatever state I am."

But notice he did not say that this sense of contentment comes naturally, as a birthright, or that it came to him as a special gift from above. (And Paul knew what it was to be struck from above; he had a personal encounter with the

Lord Jesus Christ, as described in Acts 9.) He said that contentment was something that he had *learned*.

How do we learn contentment? Strangely enough, it would seem that one way we learn contentment is through difficulties. This is what Charles Spurgeon referred to as "the college of content." Paul said he knew what it was to be in need and to have plenty, to be well-fed or hungry, to live in plenty or in want. He learned he could do all things through God who gave him strength and power.

That is true for us, too. Just as we don't learn patience without going through situations that trigger feelings of impatience, we don't learn to be truly content without trial. Paul had experienced a lifetime of trials when he wrote about contentment as an old man—in prison!

## BUT WHO WANTS FIERY TRIALS?

It is our nature—and modern society certainly encourages us—to expect life to be easy, problem-free. We think, "If I can just get past this particular barrier, everything will be smooth and serene."

So we manage to get past it, and . . . what's this? Oh, no! Another barrier!

But why are we so surprised? That's life! Or as Peter wrote, "Dear friends, do not be surprised at the painful trial you are suffering, as though something strange were happening to you" (1 Pet. 4:12).

How do we react to these trials? In *Staying Power,* Anne and Ray Ortlund speak of the "weak, chronic whiners, focusing on their problems instead of on their purposes." What purposes? The Ortlunds' model is Jesus, "who for the joy set before him endured the cross, scorning its shame" (Heb. 12:2).[2] Just as Jesus glorified God in his suffering, we are to glorify him in the sufferings of our life.

Tim Hansel, in *You Gotta Keep Dancin',* points out that, "The choice for all of us is not if we will accept pain, but *how.*" He adds, "What a test of character adversity is. It can either destroy or build up, depending on our chosen response. Pain can either make us better or bitter. . . . Pain is inevitable, misery optional."[3]

Will our pain make us better? In human sentimentality, pain may seem cruel. But God loves us so much he won't prevent the hurts that will make us grow. God is more interested in our growing into the image of Jesus Christ than he is in our comfort. We believe that our situations with our husbands are not in any sense a mistake, but that God uses our husbands to accomplish his purposes for us. As a woman who waited years for her husband's conversion declared, "It is amazing how God uses everything in my life— even my unbelieving husband—to mold me into the person he wants me to be."

*God's special work.* "Had you ever considered," a friend asked Bev, "that maybe the reason you became a Christian before your husband is that the Lord has more work to do in your life?"

This remark, made with a twinkle in the eye, may not be as flippant as it sounds. However, we would like to amend it to read "a special work," rather than "more work." God's special work is forming us into a unique vessel for his service. He is stretching our character for our highest good.

If we find ourselves wallowing in our "failure" with our husbands, we must remember that over and over again in the Bible the greatest successes were accomplished through seeming defeat.

Joseph was sold by his brothers into slavery, and then his master sent him to prison. But these were simply God's stepping-stones, preparing him in the language, culture, and politics of Egypt to rule under Pharaoh, saving the whole nation of Egypt and his family from famine.

And Jesus died the death of a criminal on the cross, to become the Savior of the world.

In *Still Higher for His Highest,* Oswald Chambers wrote about difficult circumstances that reveal the inability of our human nature. He believed that they are not calculated to make us "sink back and say, 'Oh, dear, I thought I should have been all right by now.'" They are so we will "learn to draw on our union with Jesus Christ and claim that we have sufficient grace to do this particular thing according to God's will."[4]

There's that word, *learn,* again!

*Learn to adjust our focus.* The fumes of freshly applied paint in the dental offices where Julie works made it almost impossible for her to function until a patient suggested placing a dish of vanilla in the room.

"It didn't lessen the paint smell at all," she reported. "But I could concentrate on the aroma of the vanilla instead of the paint."

We can focus on what we don't have—exemplary Christian husbands, and all the accompanying worry, fear, and anger. Or we can focus on what we do have—the comfort, peace, and security of an eternal relationship with the Lord. We tend to react to the most obvious—our circumstances. It takes effort and energy to concentrate on the Lord. But we do have a choice.

*Our husbands may keep us more dependent on God.* A friend who is an ardent deep sea fisherman calls his very active two-year-old son "the shark in the bait tank," because he keeps the household so stirred up, just as a shark would if dropped into a tank of live bait.

If your husband is like that—keeping you stirred up much of the time—could that possibly have a positive aspect? Of course it can—if it prompts you to seek the Lord and keeps you dependent on him. Thank God, then, for your own personal "shark in the bait tank!"

*Channeled water runs deeper.* Some of us feel "limited" spiritually by our marriages to unbelieving or barely believing husbands. But think for a moment what an advantage this can be. When we are limited, we are forced to seek God on how to spend the little time we have available for spiritual things. As we channel our Christian lives and our ministries under his direction, they deepen, whereas unchanneled lives may be spiritually shallow, splattering out over endless activities.[5]

Then, instead of using our husbands' lack of commitment as an excuse for not growing, we can be like Betty, who has lived nearly thirty years with a barely believing husband. Betty is convinced that she has learned more and experienced a richer, fuller Christian walk because of her marriage.

"I may not have my husband wholly and completely at my side spiritually, like many other women," she noted. "But I believe this empty spot in my life has pushed me to seek the Lord more intently. And he in turn has given me insights and discernment that many of those women haven't yet found."

Dr. James Dobson noted on a radio broadcast that three-quarters of some four hundred men and women who became major achievers in our society grew up from problem-filled childhoods. They were not limited by their backgrounds, but seemingly used them as an impetus to achieve more than those with "normal" beginnings.

Ponder that, when you are tempted to resent your limitations. So you can't reach far and wide? Reach deeper! Learn with Paul, "the depth of the riches of the wisdom and knowledge of God" (Rom. 11:33).

*Even fiery trials can bring God's good.* Listen again to Tim Hansel, who lives with constant pain. "Slowly I'm learning to trust the pain like a friend, to learn from it like a mentor, embrace it like a brother, and laugh at it like a . . . fool for Christ's sake. My eyes have been opened to see so much more of life than I would have been willing to do so otherwise. A new odyssey awaits me and I am ready for it."[6]

Our natural inclination is to run from discomfort, to avoid pain at all costs. But, like Tim Hansel, we are learning to lean into the pain—the pain of being married to an unbelieving or foot-dragging Christian husband. God has allowed it. Oh, that we may trust him enough to embrace it, to let him use it!

## "HANGETH THOU IN THERE, BABY!"

Perhaps we should make this quote from one of Kay Arthur's tapes our eleventh commandment.

Winston Churchill, who almost flunked out of Harrow, put it another way in his oft-quoted-sixteen-word speech to the students of his old alma mater.

> Young men, never give up.
> Never give up!
> Never give up!
> Never, never, never—never—never!

It is so important for us not to retreat or quit, but to keep on keeping on. Yet this isn't what our world of planned obsolescence tells us, is it?

*The world says, "Quit!"* The popular message is that if it isn't perfect, get rid of it. If it doesn't feel good, stop; get out. Don't like your job? Switch. Unplanned pregnancy? Get rid of it. Tired of your town, your house? Move. Dissatisfied with your church? Change to another. Things tough in your marriage? Divorce. Find a new mate.

Of course, there are times when change is God's perfect will for you. And we spelled out one such time when we talked about abuse in an earlier chapter. But many other times we are tempted to run when God wants us to stick it out.

We know that often it is not easy. We congratulate you for hanging in there in your marriage, and we want to encourage you to persevere.

*Ask God for "staying power."* If the time should come when you wonder if you can hang on any longer, do what Ray and Anne Ortlund suggest in *Staying Power:* "Ask God for staying power, for determination, for patience, for gutsy courage to survive and survive well."[7]

Staying power, the Ortlunds say, takes patience. "Almost everything that's terrific today, earlier wasn't. Any marriage, church, business, person, grape, tomato. Good things take time before they are good." It also requires trust.

"Waiting on him 'grows you up'; it keeps your eyes off yourself and on him; it gives you staying power."[8]

*When you get discouraged* . . . Jesus' incarnation was prophesied hundreds of years before he was born in Bethlehem. For centuries men prayed for him to come. "But when the time had fully come, God sent his Son" (Gal. 4:4). The King James Version reads: "in the fulness of time," the time God decided on.

We begin to understand then that there also will be a right time for our husbands. Solomon declared, "There is a time for everything" (Eccles. 3:1), including a time to be born. And, we would add, a time to be born again!

A few years ago, Bev's hope began to flag. She saw absolutely no spiritual progress in her husband, and one son had announced that he was thinking of taking an apartment with his girlfriend. That evening she and her husband drove to his parents' condominium. While her husband talked with his father, Mother Smith picked up a flashlight and motioned Bev out onto the second-floor balcony. She shone the light down on a tiny sprig of alyssum, growing right through the paved flooring, blooming defiantly.

"There!" she said, fixing Bev with her emphatic brown eyes, "Now, wouldn't you be ashamed ever to give up?"

*Bloom where you are planted.* It is one thing to just hang in there with white knuckles—another to thrive while waiting. Is it possible for us, like the alyssum, to bloom where we are, even if God plants us in a hard, sterile spot? Yes, it is, if we will resist the temptation to place our lives on "hold," waiting for our husbands to make a commitment to the Lord, waiting to be "free."

*Bloom with joy.* Despite constant pain, Tim Hansel wrote in *You Gotta Keep Dancin'* of realizing the incredible importance of making a commitment to joy. Without knowing or intending it, he had "put a lid on" his rage to live by telling himself that when he was strong he would be joyful or when the pain eased, he would be joyful.

He learned above all that joy didn't depend on the circumstances. In fact most frequently in Scripture it was cited as coming in spite of circumstances. He realized then it wasn't the limitations that had been imposed on him that held him back as much as his perception of those limitations. It wasn't the pain that thwarted him as much as his attitude toward the pain. "Joy," he writes, "is not a feeling; it is a choice. It is not based upon circumstances; it is based upon attitude. It is free, but it is not cheap. It is the by-product of a growing relationship with Jesus Christ."[9]

Paul was able to rejoice in his suffering for the Colossians (1:24). He challenged us to "Rejoice in the Lord always" (Phil. 4:4). Of course, we would not be rejoicing *because of* the circumstances but rejoicing *in them,* keeping the focus on God.

Oh, that we might make ourselves available to him, that his joy might remain in us and our joy might be complete! ( John 15:11)

*Decide you want to bloom.* When Bev moved "kicking and screaming" from the home she and her husband had built in the Malibu mountains overlooking the Pacific Ocean, she hated her new, viewless tract home. To remind herself that she could still be content and more, she hung a sign over her sink, "Bloom Where You are Planted." (It was while living in that tract house that she met the Lord.)

Later Anne Ortlund reminded Bev over breakfast one morning that when John was exiled to the Isle of Patmos, he could have wallowed in self-pity or stood on the shore, waiting for a ship to rescue him. Instead, he sought the Lord and was given the Book of Revelation. Now, that is blooming!

But how do we flourish despite our surroundings, despite our situation? And how do we make this more than a surface attitude, more than a cover-up for our real feelings of anger and frustration?

*We can't force the blooming.* "When the temperature reached 115 degrees in this desert town where my husband's working on his masters degree, I thought I would frizzle up and die," admitted Bev's daughter-in-law, Linda. "But I hung up your 'Bloom Where You Are Planted' sign [Bev's gift to her] and I started to do productive things like write and work on textile design. I found out that blooming can't be forced. It comes from inside. From God. And then it is an unfolding."

That inner wellspring that allows us to bloom—to open out with vigor, vitality—is the Lord Jesus Christ dwelling in us. We cannot force our growth or our maturing. It unfolds as we stop trying so hard in our own strength and let the Holy Spirit work in us.

*We need a good root system to bloom.* How do we develop this inner wellspring that allows us to bloom? To help your roots tap into his love, we say again: spend time with the Lord, get into the Bible, seek teaching in a good church, find intimate fellowship in a small prayer group or a Bible study.

And listen to Paul's prayer: "I pray that out of his glorious riches he may strengthen you with power through his Spirit in your inner being, so that Christ may dwell in your hearts through faith. And I pray that you, being rooted and established in love, may have power, together with all the saints, to grasp how wide and long and high and deep is the love of Christ, and to know this love that surpasses knowledge—that you may be filled to the measure of all the fullness of God" (Eph. 3:16-19).

Dear friends, this is our prayer for you—that you may truly comprehend the depth of God's love for you, exactly where you are right now, exactly as you are right now.

*Fragrant fruit is coming.* One summer day, David and Bryan Smith picked their mother a lovely bouquet—of tomato blossoms. Had they waited, the flowers would at first appear to shrivel. But then, slowly they would form into plump, red, ripe fruit. So take heart if there are times that you feel your "bloom" is beginning to fade. Perhaps it is just a season before it matures into fruit.

And the fruit of a flower takes many forms. Grapes, oranges, tomatoes—their blossoms are all different. But for some flowers like the orchid, the "fruit" is their beauty. And for others it is their fragrance. And Paul reminded us, "For we are to God the aroma of Christ among those who are being saved and those who are perishing" (2 Cor. 2:15). It was this fragrance to which John Henry Cardinal Newman refers in his prayer:

> Jesus, help me spread your fragrance everywhere.
> Flood my soul with Your spirit and light.
> Penetrate and possess my whole being so utterly
> that all my life may be only a reflection of Thine.
> Shine through me and be so in me
> that every soul I come in contact with
> may feel Thy presence in my soul.
> Let them look up and see no longer me but only Jesus.

Just as flowers produce different kinds of fruit, so our lives—yielded to the Holy Spirit—can produce the many varieties of the fruit of the spirit: love, joy, peace, patience, kindness, goodness, faithfulness, gentleness, self-control.

In God's plan, fruit is to be given away. The orange doesn't benefit the orange tree, but those of us who eat it. And God takes the fruit he produces in our lives and uses it to bless others.

If you will focus on the Lord—and listen—there is no telling what fruit, what fragrance he might grow through you to bless others. Be open. Be receptive. Be willing. Your life can glorify God right now.

"Who, me?" you say. "I don't see how."

*Your trust glorifies God.* Paul wrote, paying tribute to Abraham's faith, noting that God promised to give the whole earth to Abraham and his descendants, not because Abraham obeyed God's laws but because he trusted God to keep his promise. Despite his circumstances, Abraham believed God's promise and "was strengthened in his faith and gave glory to God" (Rom. 4:20).

We have seen throughout this book that God has given us many promises regarding our marriages to unbelieving or barely believing husbands. If we, like Abraham, can have faith in what God has promised, then we, too, give glory to God!

*You glorify God in your marriage.* Do you fall into the trap of thinking, "My marriage will glorify God when my husband becomes a committed believer"?

Wrong! Today, this very moment, your marriage glorifies God.

Think about it. That which glorifies God is not the perfect situation, but how his people handle an imperfect situation. This also can be the best witness to others.

Many years ago, Dottie sought the Lord concerning her husband's salvation. And the Lord asked her, "Would you be willing to spend the rest of your life showing your husband Jesus' love and caring?"

Her answer was, "Yes, Lord."

And just recently she told Pat, "I believe that God, right this moment, is getting glory from my relationship with my husband."

And the people of her church bear witness to this. Woman after woman told Pat she must talk to Dottie before we finished this book, because she has such a reputation as a godly woman who has raised two godly children.

We think Dottie is a good example of what Paul wrote: "our light, momentary troubles are achieving for us an eternal glory" (2 Cor. 9:17).

So as we wait, and trust, and honor him, as we love our husbands unconditionally—not because they are such wonderful Christians, but because they are our husbands—our marriages too can glorify God.

We pray that we may each learn to be content, to know that God has blessed us by putting us right where we are, and that God is working all our struggles together for our good and for His glory.

## QUESTIONS FOR FURTHER STUDY
## AND GROUP DISCUSSION

1. Reread the definitions of contentment in the chapter and then define it in your own words. Give an example of an area of your life where you are content, although not necessarily happy.

2. Look up the following passages where contentment is mentioned:

> *Philippians 4:4-13*
> *1 Timothy 6:3-12*
> *Hebrews 13:5-6*

Do you agree with the chapter that learning contentment often involves trials? Why? Are there other ways of learning contentment?

3. Read *1 Corinthians 7:13-24*. How do you bloom where you are planted or thrive in the circumstances in which you find yourself? List the ideas in the chapter, then add your own. To encourage one another, share some personal examples of blooming in adverse circumstances.

4. Read the following verses:

> *Hebrews 12:1b-12*
> *James 1:2-5, 12*

Have you tried choosing joy in difficult situations? Give an example. Was it just a mask you put on for others or were you able to experience yourself? What helped you move from negative attitudes into joy?

5. Read *Romans 8:28*. How might our concept of good differ from God's? When will this working of all things for good be accomplished? Does this verse provide help in your difficulties now? Does it give you hope, something to look forward to in the future?

6. In what ways does your life and your marriage glorify God now? What fruit do you have in your life and marriage for others to pick? Share how you have been blessed by the marriages of others, especially those in your group.

7. Are you content in your marriage, in your life now? With what areas are you still struggling? Can you trust God to teach you, to help you learn to be content? Then ask him!

8. What have you learned in this book that has helped you be more content?

**Pray again for your husbands and then ask the Lord to be with each of you in your trials and to help you learn contentment.**

# NOTES

**CHAPTER ONE**
1. David Claerbaut, *Liberation from Loneliness* (Wheaton, Ill.: Tyndale, 1984), 10.
2. Tim Timmons, *Loneliness Is Not a Disease* (Eugene, Oreg.: Harvest House, 1981), 54-55.
3. Claerbaut, 40.
4. Archibald D. Hart, *Feeling Free* (Old Tappan, N.J.: Revell, 1979), 52.
5. W. Peter Blitchington, *Sex Roles and the Christian Family* (Wheaton, Ill.: Tyndale, 1980), 53-54.
6. Cited in Beverly Beyette, "The Battle of the Sexes," *Los Angeles Times,* 25 September 1985, Part V, 1, 4.

**CHAPTER TWO**
1. Elisabeth Elliot, *The Mark of a Man* (Old Tappan, N.J.: Revell, 1981), 24.
2. Blitchington, 53-54.
3. Melvin Konner, "She & He," *Science 82,* 57; Blitchington, 50-53.
4. Blitchington, 50-53.
5. Elizabeth Mehren, "Two Looks at Male, Female Friendship," *Los Angeles Times,* 8 June 1983, Part V, 1-2.
6. Joyce Brothers, *What Every Woman Should Know about*

*Men* (New York: Simon and Schuster, 1981), 111.
7. Konner, 57; Blitchington, 50–53.
8. Blitchington, 53–54.
9. Ibid.
10. S. Bruce Narramore, *No Condemnation* (Grand Rapids, Mich.: Academie Books, Zondervan, 1984), 264.

**CHAPTER THREE**
1. W. E. Vine, *Vine's Expository Dictionary of Old and New Testament Words* (Old Tappan, N.J.: Revell, 1981), 152.

**CHAPTER FOUR**
1. Claerbaut, 70.

**CHAPTER FIVE**
1. Vine, 9.
2. *Los Angeles Times,* Part V, 2 June 1986, 1.
3. Brother Lawrence, *Practice of the Presence of God* (Old Tappan, N.J.: Revell, 1958), 30.
4. Frank C. Lauback, *Open Windows, Swinging Doors* (Glendale, Calif.: Regal, 1955), 10–11, 76.
5. Oswald Chambers, *Still Higher for His Highest* (Grand Rapids, Mich.: Zondervan, 1970), 29.
6. Kay Arthur, video Bible study on the Sermon on the Mount (Chattanooga, Tenn.: Precept Ministries).
7. Shannon Gustafson, Bible study on intercessory prayer (Costa Mesa, Calif.: Newport Mesa Christian Center, 1985–86).
8. Hazel McAlister, *No Pat Answers* (Nashville: Abingdon, 1986), 37.

**CHAPTER SIX**
1. Brothers, 245.
2. Blitchington, 57.
3. James Strong, *Strong's Exhaustive Concordance of the Bible* (Nashville: Abingdon, 1980), 87.
4. Strong, 60.

5. Strong, 35.
6. F. B. Meyer, *Tried by Fire* (Fort Washington, Penn.: Christian Literature Crusade, n.d.), 100.
7. Gary Smalley, *The Joy of Committed Love* (Grand Rapids: Zondervan, 1984), 268.
8. Anne Ortlund, *Building a Great Marriage* (Old Tappan, N.J.: Revell, 1985), 60.

CHAPTER EIGHT

1. "Why Men Hurt the Women They Love," *Reader's Digest,* January 1986, 77.
2. "Counselor Says Wife Abuse Happens in Every Church," *Charisma,* July 1987, 54.
3. James Monte Alsdurf, *Wife Abuse and the Christian Faith,* doctoral dissertation, Fuller Theological Seminary, 1951, 31.
4. Based on interviews with Gillian Martin, counselor at the Women's Transitional Living Center, a shelter for abused women in Orange County, California, and staff from other shelters in southern California.
5. Lenore E. Walker, *The Battered Woman* (New York: Harper & Row, 1979), 31, 36.
6. Strong, 45.
7. Esther Lee Olson with Kenneth Petersen, *No Place to Hide* (Wheaton, Ill.: Tyndale, 1982), 135.
8. "Stopping the Wife-Beating Cycle," *Los Angeles Times,* 20 December 1985, Part V, 46–47.
9. "Why Men Hurt the Women They Love," 77–81.

CHAPTER NINE

1. Ross Campbell, *How to Really Love Your Child* (Wheaton, Ill.: Victor Books, 1980), 125–126.
2. Virginia Hearn, *What They Did Right* (Wheaton, Ill.: Tyndale, 1974), 226.
3. Nancy L. Nehmer, *A Parent's Guide to Christian Books for Children* (Wheaton, Ill.: Tyndale, 1984).
4. Hearn, 258–259.

5. Copyright 1982 by *Guideposts* magazine, Guideposts Associates, Inc., Carmel, N.Y.

CHAPTER ELEVEN

1. W. E. Vine, *Vine's Expository Dictionary of Old and New Testament Words* (Old Tappan, N.J.: Revell, 1981), 234.
2. Ray and Anne Ortlund, *Staying Power* (Nashville: Thomas Nelson, 1986), 64.
3. Tim Hansel, *You Gotta Keep Dancin'* (Elgin, Ill.: David C. Cook, 1985) 35, 39, 55.
4. Chambers, 17.
5. Hansel, 94.
6. Hansel, 44.
7. Ortlund, 103.
8. Ortlund, 49.
9. Hansel, 46–48, 54–55.